FINANCIAL ENGLISH

with Mini-Dictionary of Finance

Ian MacKenzie

ACHING PUBLICATIONS
2BE, England

ISBN 1 899396 00 4
© LTP 1995
NO UNAUTHORISED PHOTOCOPYING

Copyright

The Author

Ian MacKenzie has taught English in London, New York and Switzerland. He is currently teaching in the School of Business and Economics at Lausanne University.

Acknowledgements

The author would like to thank Jimmie Hill, Michael Lewis, and Mark Powell for helpful suggestions; and Simone Westerhuis for checking the exercises and answer key.

Cover design by Anna Macleod
Cover photograph by Richard Einzig/Arcaid
Cartoons by Charles Peattie and Russell Taylor and Punch
Typeset by Blackmore Typesetting Services, Brighton
Printed in England by Commercial Colour Press, London E7
Reprinted 1996

Using this Book

WHO IS THIS BOOK FOR?

This book is for anyone working or planning to work in the field of finance who wants to be able to discuss financial matters, read the financial press, or consult financial documents with greater ease and confidence. The units take you step by step through the whole world of finance, giving you the essential language and terminology you need. Separate sections deal with:

1. **Talking Figures**
2. **Accounting Basics**
3. **Money and Banking**
4. **Trade and Commerce**
5. **Company Finance**
6. **Economic Issues**

It is a good idea to begin with Section 1 because you will want to be able to present and understand figures in English – no matter what area of finance you are interested in.

IF YOU WORK IN FINANCE ALREADY

You will find it helpful to go through Sections 2 - 6 in the contents list, underline the most useful units, and work on these first. If your job is highly specialised, you may want to work in depth on the section that is most relevant to your professional needs. On the other hand, if your job carries more general responsibilities, you may prefer to do two or three units in one section and then move on to another.

IF YOU ARE STUDYING FOR A CAREER IN FINANCE

If you have little or no professional experience, it is best to work through the sections systematically. Much of the language is recycled and there are Review Units in each section to revise the most important new vocabulary. For you, Section 6, Economic Issues, is a good place to begin. This will give you a background in basic economic theory. You can then choose whichever section interests you most and do that next.

IF YOU ARE USING THIS BOOK ON YOUR OWN

Try to set aside half an hour twice a week for study. This is much better than doing nothing for weeks and then trying to study for a whole evening. One unit is usually sufficient for one study session. You will find the answers to all the exercises in the answer key at the back of the book. When you complete a unit, always read through it again a day or two later. This is the best way to make sure you do not forget the new language.

IF YOU ARE USING THIS BOOK WITH A TEACHER IN CLASS

Make sure you explain to your teacher exactly what your job involves, so that you can decide together which parts of the book to study first and in what order. If possible, work with a partner on the exercises. Where the units contain longer texts, it may be better to do these at home and bring your notes to the next class to discuss with your teacher.

THE MINI-DICTIONARY

If you have problems doing any of the exercises, the mini-dictionary at the back of the book will help you. Good luck with your studies!

Talking Figures

"If you can actually count your money,
then you are not really a rich man."
JOHN PAUL GETTY

Numbers and You

Most people working in finance, whether it is in accountancy, banking, broking, investment, insurance, or whatever, spend a lot of time dealing with numbers. Reading, hearing, saying, writing, numbers in a foreign language generally requires practice.

When do you need to work with numbers?

1. I work in . . . .

2. I need the English of Finance for . . . .

I regularly read numbers in English in:

1. textbooks
2. newspapers
3. magazines and journals

4. accounts
5. company documents
6. . . . .

I hear numbers spoken in English when . . . .

I have to use numbers in English:

1. in the classroom
2. in meetings

3. on the phone
4. . . . .

in order to:

. . . .

. . . .

Tick which of the following you have to do in English:

1. buy goods or services over the telephone
2. describe graphs
3. discuss accounts
4. discuss customers' bank accounts
5. discuss projects with colleagues
6. discuss the market price of securities
7. draw up budgets
8. negotiate with producers, customers, brokers, etc.
9. present accounts and results to managers, colleagues, shareholders
10. present products or services to customers
11. sell products or services over the telephone
12. talk with technicians

Saying Numbers

1. OH, ZERO, LOVE, NOUGHT, NIL!

The above are all ways of saying 0 in English.

We say **oh**	after a decimal point	5.03	five point oh three
	in telephone numbers	67 01 38	six seven oh one three eight
	in bus numbers	No. 701	get the seven oh one
	in hotel room numbers	Room 206	I'm in room two oh six.
	in years	1905	nineteen oh five
We say **nought**	before the decimal point	0.02	nought point oh two
We say **zero**	for the number	0	the number zero
	for temperature	–5°C	five degrees below zero
We say **nil**	in football scores	5–0	Spain won five nil.
We say **love**	in tennis	15–0	The score is fifteen love.

Now say the following:

1. The exact figure is 0.002.
2. Can you get back to me on 01244 249071? I'll be here all morning.
3. Can you put that on my bill? I'm in room 804.
4. Do we have to hold the conference in Reykjavik? It's 30 degrees below 0!
5. What's the score? 2–0 to Juventus.

2. THE DECIMAL POINT

In English, we use a point (.) and not a comma (,) for decimals. We use commas in figures only when writing thousands.

> 10,001 is ten thousand and one.
> 10.001 is ten point oh oh one.

> When accounts are prepared on computer, commas are not used. The number appears as 82103.

In English all the numbers after a decimal point are read separately:

10.66	**ten point six six**	Not ten point sixty six
0.325	**nought point three two five**	
0.001	**nought point oh oh one**	or 10^{-3}, ten to the power minus three

You will also hear people say:

| 0.05 | **zero point oh five** | or **oh point oh five** |

But if the number after the decimal point is a unit of money, it is read like a normal number:

| £12.50 | **twelve pounds fifty** | DM 2.95 | **two marks ninety five** |

NB. This is very important. When you do business on the phone, say **nought point three seven five** (0.375) and **not** nought point three hundred and seventy five. If the listener missed the word point, you might lose a lot of money. Say the digits separately after the point.

Now say the following:

1. It's somewhere between 3.488 and 3.491.
2. Look, it's less than 0.0001! It's hardly worth worrying about.
3. I changed all those lira into sterling and I only got £13.60!
4. That's about 14.50 in Swiss francs.
5. Did you say 0.225 or 0.229?
6. The dollar is at 1.95.
7. No, I meant 15.005 not 15,005.

3. PER CENT

The stress is on the cent of per cent   ten perCENT

Notice the following when talking about interest rates:

0.5%   a half of one per cent

0.25%   a quarter of a percentage point

For example:

The Bank of England raised interest rates this morning by a quarter of a percentage point.

Now say the following:

1. What's 30% of 260?
2. They have put the rate up by another 0.5%.
3. 0.75% won't make a lot of difference.

4. HUNDREDS, THOUSANDS, AND MILLIONS

In British English you hear	**a hundred and twenty three.**
In American English you usually hear	**a hundred twenty three.**
The number 1,999 is said	**one thousand nine hundred and ninety nine.**
The year 1999 is said	**nineteen ninety nine.**
The year 2000 is said	**the year two thousand.**
The year 2001 is said	**two thousand and one.**
The year 2015 is said	**two thousand and fifteen or twenty fifteen.**

Note: It is likely that different people will refer to the early years of the 21st century in different ways. Remember that the year 1066 is always referred to as ten sixty six – not one thousand and sixty six.

1,000,000	is **a million** or ten to the power six. (10^6)
1,000,000,000	is **a billion** or ten to the power nine. (10^9)

This is now common usage. British English used to be that a billion was ten to the power twelve (10^{12}), but now everyone has accepted the current American usage.

Now say the following:

1. Why do you say 175 in Britain? In the States we usually say 175.
2. It's got 1001 different uses.
3. Profits will have doubled by the year 2000.
4. Thanks. You're one in 1,000,000!
5. No, that's 2,000,000,000 not 2,000,000!

5. SQUARES, CUBES, AND ROOTS

10^2 is ten squared.

10^3 is ten cubed.

$\sqrt{6}$ is the square root of 6.

6. TELEPHONE AND FAX NUMBERS

We usually give telephone and fax numbers as individual digits:

01273 736344	**oh one two seven three, seven three six, three four four**
344	can also be said as **three double four**
44 26 77	**double four, two six, double seven**
777	can be said as **seven double seven,** or **seven seven seven**

7. FRACTIONS

Fractions are mostly like ordinal numbers (fifth, sixth, twenty third etc):

a third	**a fifth**	**a sixth**

Notice, however, the following:

a half	**a quarter**	**three quarters**
three and a half	**two and three quarters**	

Now read the following news item:

> In an opinion poll published today, over $3/4$ of the electorate say they intend to vote in next month's referendum. $1/4$ of voters say they will definitely vote Yes, while $1/3$ will vote No. But that leaves over $2/5$ of the voters who haven't made up their minds. Both sides remain hopeful. A spokesman for the 'Yes' campaign said, "At the moment, $2/3$ of the electorate won't vote No." A spokeswoman for the other side replied, "That's true, but $3/4$ won't vote Yes!"

8. CALCULATING

Remember to pronounce the *s* in *equals* as /z/. It is singular; the part on the left **equals** the part on the right.

$10 + 4 = 14$	ten **plus** four is fourteen
	ten **and** four equals fourteen
$10 - 4 = 6$	ten **minus** four is six
	ten **take away** four equals six
$10 \times 4 = 40$	ten **times** four is (or equals) forty
	ten **multiplied by** four is forty
$10 \div 4 = 2^{1}/_{2}$	ten **divided by** four is two and a half

+ = **add**	− = **subtract** (or **deduct**)	× = **multiply**	÷ = **divide**

Other ways of saying divide are:

per	Fr/$	**francs per dollar**
	6% p.a.	**six per cent per annum**
over	$(x - y)/z$	**x minus y, over z** which is not the
		same as **x, minus y over z:** $x - y/z$

9. FOREIGN CURRENCY

Notice these ways of speaking about exchange rates:

How many **francs** are there **to the dollar**?

How many **francs per dollar** did you get?

The current rate is **205 pesetas to the pound.**

How would you say these dollar rates?

DOLLAR RATES	
Australia	1.4060-1.4070
Canada	1.3756-1.3766
France	4.8520-4.8540
Germany	1.3843-1.3848
Hong Kong	7.7360-7.7370
Japan	84.96-85.01

10. NUMBERS AS ADJECTIVES

When a number is used before a noun – like an adjective – it is always singular. We say:

a fifty-minute lesson   **not** a fifty-minutes lesson

Here are more examples:

a sixteen-week semester   a thirty-five pound book

a fifteen-minute walk   a six-week waiting list

a twenty-pound reduction   a two and a half litre bottle

a six billion dollar loan   a two litre engine

Say the following in a similar way:

1. They lent us £250,000.   They gave us a . . . .

2. Our house is 200 years old.   We bought a . . . .

3. We lost $50,000.   We made a . . . .

4. The salmon weighed 15 pounds!   I caught a . . . .

11. REVIEW

How many of the following can you say aloud in under 1 minute?

1. 234, 567

2. 1,234,567,890

3. 1.234

4. 0.00234%

5. 3.14159

6. $19.50

7. £7.95

8. 19, 999

9. 1, 999 years

10. In 1999

11. I think the phone number is 01227–764000.

12. Have you got a pen? Their fax number is: 00 33 567 32 49.

13. Please pay it into my account – number G4.744.440.

14. He was born in 1905 and died in 1987.

15. It's a white Lamborghini Diabolo, registration number MI 234662, and it looks as if it's doing 225 kilometres an hour!

16. $30 \times 25 = 750$

17. $30 \div 25 = 1.20$

18. $x^2 + y^3 = z$

Accounting Basics

"With 'creative accountancy', who needs cheating?"
KATHARINE WHITEHORN

Company Law

Complete the text using the words in the box:

bankruptcy	corporations	creditors	issue	liability
losses	partnership	registered	shares	sole trader
financial	premises	capital	prospectus	files

TYPES OF BUSINESS

The simplest form of business is the individual proprietorship or (1) . . . .: for example, a shop (US = store) or a taxi owned by a single person. If several individuals wish to go into business together they can form a (2) . . . .; partners generally contribute equal capital, have equal authority in management, and share profits or (3) . . . . In many countries, lawyers, doctors and accountants are not allowed to form companies, but only partnerships with unlimited (4) . . . . for debts – which should make them act responsibly.

But a partnership is not a legal entity separate from its owners; like sole traders, partners have unlimited liability: in the case of (5) . . . ., a partner with a personal fortune can lose it all. Consequently, the majority of businesses are limited companies (US = (6) . . . .), in which investors are only liable for the amount of capital they have invested. If a limited company goes bankrupt, its assets are sold (liquidated) to pay the debts; if the assets do not cover the debts, they remain unpaid (i.e. (7) . . . . do not get their money back.)

In Britain, most smaller enterprises are private limited companies which cannot offer (8) . . . . to the public; their owners can only raise capital from friends or from banks and other venture capital institutions. A successful, growing British business can apply to the Stock Exchange to become a public limited company; if accepted, it can publish a (9) . . . . and offer its shares for sale on the open stock market. In America, there is no legal distinction between private and public limited corporations, but the equivalent of a public limited company is one (10) . . . . by the Securities and Exchange Commission.

FOUNDING A COMPANY

Founders of companies have to write a Memorandum of Association (in the US, a Certificate of Incorporation), which states the company's name, purpose, registered office or premises and authorised share (11) . . . .

(12). . . . . (always with an 's' at the end) – is the technical term for the place in which a company does its business: an office, a shop, a workshop, a factory, a warehouse, etc. Authorised share capital means the maximum amount of a particular type of share the company can (13) . . . .

Founders also write Articles of Association (US = Bylaws), which set out the rights and duties of directors and different classes of shareholders. Companies' memoranda and articles of association, and annual (14). . . . . statements are sent to the registrar of companies, where they may be inspected by the public. (A company that (15) . . . . its financial statements late is almost certainly in trouble.) In Britain, founders can buy a ready-made "off-the-shelf" company from an agent, that is, a company formed and held specifically for later resale; the buyer then changes the name, memorandum, and so on.

Notice that the verb here is to *found* a company. This regular verb (found-founded-founded) should not be confused with the irregular verb to *find* (find-found-found).

Bookkeeping

EXERCISE 1

Complete the text using these words:

credits	**debits**	**double-entry**	**invoice**
journals	**ledger**	**posted**	**receipt**
transactions	**transferred**	**trial balance**	**vouchers**

Bookkeepers record every purchase and sale that a business makes, in the order that they take place, in (1) . . . . At a later date, these temporary records are entered in or (2) . . . . to the relevant account book or (3) . . . . Of course the "books" these days are likely to be computer files. At the end of an accounting period, all the relevant totals are (4) . . . . to the profit and loss account. (5) . . . . bookkeeping records the dual effect of every transaction – a value both received and parted with. Payments made or (6) . . . . are entered on the left-hand (debtor) side of an account, and payments received or (7) . . . . on the right-hand side. Bookkeepers will periodically do a (8) . . . . to test whether both sides of an account book match. In most business (9) . . . ., the seller of goods or services sends the buyer a bill or (10) . . . ., and later a (11) . . . . acknowledging payment. Businesses are obliged to retain the documents – known as (12) . . . . – that support or prove an item in an account, and make them available to the internal and external auditors who check the accounts. Bookkeepers are not to be confused with librarians, who also keep books, or with bookmakers, who "make books" in the sense that they accept bets (on horse races, etc.) and traditionally wrote them down in a book like a bookkeeper's journal. Accountants, unlike bookkeepers, analyse financial records, and decide how to present them.

EXERCISE 2

Add appropriate verbs from the text above to these sentences:

1. Bookkeepers . . . . business transactions.

2. A debit is a payment . . . .

3. A credit is a payment . . . .

4. Debits are . . . . on the left-hand side.

5. At the bottom of the page, bookkeepers . . . . the totals.

6. Companies have to . . . . invoices and receipts.

7. The auditors . . . . the accounts.

8. Accountants, managers and shareholders . . . . the accounts.

Accounting

Match the remarks on the left with the responses on the right:

1. You're an accountant? Does that mean you spend your time writing down credits and debits, and adding up columns of figures all day? Can't be very exciting.

   a. Ha! Now you're going to ask me to tell you how you can pay less tax.

2. So what do accountants do?

   b. No, managerial accountants do, but I work in cost accounting. We have to work out the real cost of each item the company makes, which means finding a way to allocate all the overheads to different products.

3. You mean the shareholders?

   c. No, not only. Managers always need the help of accountants. They need financial statements, and budgets, and cash-flow projections, and so on, to measure the success of what they've done, and to make decisions about allocating resources for future projects.

4. So you prepare reports for managers?

   d. Of course. But like I said, we're necessary. And useful. Haven't you heard of "window dressing"?

5. And the cost of the accounts department!

   e. Sure, but it's also another name for what some people call "creative accounting" – making a company's financial situation look as good as possible in the balance sheet, and so on. It's not very legal, but it happens. The accountants in my firm also have lots of wonderful ways of reducing our tax bill.

6. You mean what they do in the front of shops?

   f. That's bookkeeping. Not quite the same thing.

7. Ah, now *that's* interesting...

   g. Well, accountants do record cash flows, and the value of assets and liabilities, and they calculate profits and losses, and so on. But it's not just writing down numbers. We're really in the business of supplying people with information.

8. Not at all. As a matter of fact, I'm a tax inspector...

1	2	3	4	5	6	7	

Accounting Principles 1

There are various possible ways of recording debits and credits, valuing assets and liabilities, calculating profits and losses, etc. But there are about a dozen generally accepted "accounting principles" that accountants must follow in order to present "a true and fair view" of a company's finances.

EXERCISE 1

Match up these six accounting principles with the definitions below:

1. The separate-entity or accounting entity assumption
2. The continuity or going-concern assumption
3. The unit-of-measure assumption
4. The time-period or accounting period assumption
5. The historical cost principle
6. The revenue or realization principle

a. All transactions and other items to be accounted for must be in a single, supposedly stable monetary unit.

b. An enterprise is an accounting unit separate from its owners, creditors, etc.

c. Financial data must be reported for particular (short) periods, which makes accrual and deferral necessary.

d. Revenue is realized at the moment when goods are sold (or change hands) or when services are rendered.

e. The business will continue indefinitely into the future.

f. The initial price paid for the acquisition of assets is the one that is recorded in accounts.

1		2		3		4		5		6	

EXERCISE 2

Which principles do these sentences refer to?

1. This accords with a company's legal status as an artificial person.

2. This implies that the current market value of fixed assets is irrelevant, as they are not for sale.

3. This makes it unnecessary to estimate current market values every year.

4. This means that each company has its own financial year (US: fiscal year).

5. This requires multinational companies to convert their consolidated statements into a single currency.

6. This is why balance sheets often contain an entry for debtors: goods that have been sold, but are not yet paid for.

Accounting Principles 2

EXERCISE 1

Match up these five accounting principles with the definitions below:

1. The matching principle

2. The objectivity principle

3. The consistency principle

4. The full-disclosure principle

5. The principle of conservatism (or prudence)

a. All data recorded should be verifiable and free from bias.

b. Financial reporting must include all significant information.

c. The revenues generated in an accounting period are identified with related costs whenever they were incurred.

d. The same methods (of inventory valuation, depreciation, etc.) must be used from one period to the next.

e. Where alternative accounting methods are possible, one understates rather than overstates profits.

1		2		3		4	·	5	

EXERCISE 2

Which principles do these sentences refer to?

1. This is the contrary of recording "below-the-line" items.

2. This is one of the justifications for historical cost accounting, which requires no subjective assessments of replacement values.

3. This leads to the accrual (accumulation) and deferral (postponement) of costs.

4. This means that *insignificant* trivial expenses, like each pencil or typewriter ribbon, need not be accounted for separately, but are exempted by the principle of materiality.

5. This prevents companies selecting methods according to the inflation rate, etc.

Types of Assets

Match these accounting terms with the definitions below, and then use five of them to label the drawings:

current or **circulating** or **floating assets**

fixed or **capital** or **permanent assets**

intangible assets

liquid or **available assets**

net assets

net current assets or **working capital**

wasting assets

1. . . . . are anything that can quickly be turned into cash.

2. . . . . are the excess of current assets (such as cash, inventories, debtors) over current liabilities (creditors, overdrafts, etc.).

3. . . . . are those which are gradually exhausted (used up) in production and cannot be replaced.

4. . . . . are those which will be consumed or turned into cash in the ordinary course of business.

5. . . . . are those whose value can only be quantified or turned into cash with difficulty, such as goodwill, patents, copyrights and trade marks.

6. . . . . , or shareholders' equity, on a business's balance sheet, is assets minus liabilities (which is generally equal to fixed assets plus the difference between current assets and current liabilities).

7. . . . . , such as land, buildings and machines, cannot be sold or turned into cash, as they are required for making and selling the firm's products.

Now label each picture with the appropriate term:

Valuable reputation
The Brighton-based independent ELT publisher LTP seems to go from strength to strength, based largely on its reputation for innovation – a quality its entrepreneurial founders work hard to protect.

| 8. . . . . | 9. . . . . | 10. . . . . | 11. . . . . | 12. . . . . |

Depreciation

EXERCISE 1

Complete the text by inserting the correct form of the verbs in the box:

allow	charge	deduct	encourage
exist	increase	involve	lose
convert	spread	wear out	write off

Fixed assets such as buildings, plant and machinery (but not land) gradually (1) . . . . value, because they (2) . . . . or decay, or because more modern and efficient versions are developed. Consequently, they have to be replaced every so often. The cost of buying or replacing fixed assets that will be used over many years is not (3) . . . . from a single year's profits but is accounted for over the several years of their use and wearing out. This accords with the matching principle that costs are identified with related revenues. The process of (4) . . . . an asset into an expense is known as depreciation.

Various methods of depreciation (5) . . . . , but they all (6) . . . . estimating the useful life of the asset, and dividing its estimated cost (e.g. purchase price minus any scrap or second-hand value at the end of its useful life) by the number of years. The most usual method of depreciation is the straight line method, which simply spreads the total expected cost over the number of years of anticipated useful life, and charges an equal sum each year. The reducing or declining balance method (7). . . . . smaller amounts of an asset's value each year in cases where maintenance costs for the use of an asset are expected to (8) . . . . over time. The annuity system of depreciation (9) . . . . the cost of an asset equally over a number of years and (10) . . . . this, and an amount representing the interest on the asset's current value, each year.

Some tax legislations (11) . . . . accelerated depreciation: writing off large amounts of the cost of capital investments during the first years of use; this is a measure to (12) . . . . investment.

NOTE

In the US, the word *amortization* is sometimes used instead of *depreciation*.

EXERCISE 2

Add appropriate words to these sentences:

1.   A worn out or obsolete machine has to be . . . .

2.   Land, unlike machines, usually appreciates – i.e. it . . . . in value.

3.   To depreciate an asset accurately, you have to . . . . its useful life.

4.   The materials that make up an obsolete machine can be recycled if it is sold for . . . .

5.   A percentage of the value of fixed assets is . . . . against or . . . . from the profits, and becomes a source of funds.

6 .   Writing off value means . . . . it.

7.   Keeping a machine in good working condition is called . . . .

8.   Accelerated depreciation allows firms that make capital investments to pay less . . . .

Cash Flow

EXERCISE 1

Insert the following words in the gaps in the text:

insolvent	liquidity	net	positive
reputation	reserves	suppliers	working

Cash flow is essentially a company's ability to earn cash. It is the amount of cash made during a specified period that a business can use for investment. (More technically, it is (1) . . . . profit plus depreciation plus variations in (2) . . . .) The flow of funds is cash received and payments made by a company during a specific period – except that many people also use the term cash flow to describe this! New companies generally begin with adequate funds or (3) . . . . capital for the introductory stage during which they make contacts, find customers and build up sales and a (4) . . . . But when sales begin to rise, companies often run out of working capital: their cash is all tied up in work-in-progress, stocks and credit to customers. It is an unfortunate fact of business life that while (5) . . . . tend to demand quick payment, customers usually insist on extended credit, so the more you sell, the more cash you need. This provokes a typical (6) . . . . crisis: the business does not have enough cash to pay short-term expenses. A (7) . . . . cash flow will only reappear when sales growth slows down and the company stops "overtrading". But companies that have not arranged sufficient credit will not get this far: they will find themselves (8) . . . . – unable to meet their liabilities.

NOTE

In the US the word *inventory* is used instead of *stock(s)*.

EXERCISE 2

Match up these words to make word partnerships from Exercise 1, then match them with the definitions below:

1. extended
2. working
3. cash
4. net
5. liquidity

a. capital
b. profit
c. crisis
d. credit
e. received

i.   money already paid
ii. the money and stocks of goods held by a company which are used to produce more goods and to continue trading
iii. longer than normal payment terms
iv. short of cash
v.   the money made from selling goods after the deduction of all associated costs

1		2		3		4		5		

Financial Statements

EXERCISE 1

Which eight of the following sixteen words would you expect to find in a short text defining the different financial statements?

balance	**bookkeeping**	**bookmaking**	**capital**
capitalist	**equilibrium**	**flow**	**liabilities**
limited liability	**overheads**	**overturn**	**pour**
reservations	**reserves**	**turnover**	**underground**

Now read the text, and underline the eight words you chose above:

Companies are required by law to give their shareholders certain financial information. Most companies include three financial statements in their annual reports.

The profit and loss account shows revenue and expenditure. It gives figures for total sales or turnover (the amount of business done by the company during the year), and for costs and overheads. The first figure should be greater than the second: there should generally be a profit – an excess of income over expenditure. Part of the profit is paid to the government in taxation, part is usually distributed to shareholders as a dividend, and part is retained by the company to finance further growth, to repay debts, to allow for future losses, and so on.

The balance sheet shows the financial situation of the company on a particular date, generally the last day of its financial year. It lists the company's assets, its liabilities, and shareholders' funds. A business's assets consist of its cash investments and property (buildings, machines, and so on), and debtors – amounts of money owed by customers for goods or services purchased on credit. Liabilities consist of all the money that a company will have to pay to someone else, such as taxes, debts, interest and mortgage payments, as well as money owed to suppliers for purchases made on credit, which are grouped together on the balance sheet as creditors. Negative items on financial statements such as creditors, taxation, and dividends paid are usually printed in brackets thus: (5200).

The basic accounting equation, in accordance with the principle of double-entry bookkeeping, is that Assets = Liabilities + Owners' (or Shareholders') Equity. This can, of course, also be written as Assets – Liabilities = Equity. An alternative term for Shareholders' Equity is Net Assets. This includes share capital (money received from the issue of shares), sometimes share premium (money realized by selling shares at above their nominal value), and the company's reserves, including the year's retained profits. A company's market capitalization – the total value of its shares at any given moment, equal to the number of shares times their market price – is generally higher than shareholders' equity or net assets, because items such as goodwill are not recorded under net assets.

A third financial statement has several names: the source and application of funds statement, the sources and uses of funds statement, the funds flow statement, the cash flow statement, the movements of funds statement, or in the USA the statement of changes in financial position. As all these alternative names suggest, this statement shows the flow of cash in and out of the business between balance sheet dates. Sources of funds include trading profits, depreciation provisions, borrowing, the sale of assets, and the issuing of shares. Applications of funds include the purchase of fixed or financial assets, the payment of dividends and the repayment of loans, and, in a bad year, trading losses.

If a company has a majority interest in other companies, the balance sheets and profit and loss accounts of the parent company and the subsidiaries are normally combined in consolidated accounts.

EXERCISE 2

According to the text, are the following TRUE or FALSE?

1. Company profits are generally divided three ways. TRUE/FALSE

2. Balance sheets show a company's financial situation on 31 December. TRUE/FALSE

3. The totals in balance sheets generally include sums of money that have not yet been paid. TRUE/FALSE

4. Assets are what you own; liabilities are what you owe. TRUE/FALSE

5. Ideally, managers would like financial statements to contain no items in brackets. TRUE/FALSE

6. Limited companies cannot make a loss because assets always equal shareholders' equity. TRUE/FALSE

7. A company's shares are often worth more than its assets. TRUE/FALSE

8. The two sides of a funds flow statement show trading profits and losses. TRUE/FALSE

9. Depreciation is a source rather than a use of funds. TRUE/FALSE

10. A consolidated account is a combination of a balance sheet and a profit and loss account. TRUE/FALSE

EXERCISE 3

The text above contains various British terms that are not used in the USA. Match up the following British and American terms:

British	American
1. creditors	a. accounts payable
2. debtors	b. accounts receivable
3. overheads	c. income statement
4. profit and loss account	d. overhead
5. shareholder	e. paid-in surplus
6. share premium	f. stockholder

1		2		3		4		5		6	

Liquid Metaphors

EXERCISE 1

Cash flow, source of funds, liquid assets... . Financial English uses a lot of metaphors based on liquids. Complete the sentences below using these words in the correct form:

verbs:	channel	dry up	flood	flow
	pour	run out of	swim	trickle down
nouns:	drain	ebb and flow	pool	source
adjective:	awash			

1. After the merger, the new company will be able to draw on a huge . . . . of resources.
2. Because of the new high interest rates, money is . . . . into Germany.
3. If we don't find a new . . . . of funds, we are going to . . . . money by Christmas.
4. If private funding really does . . . . , we will have to turn to the government for help.
5. Right-wing governments tend to argue that if you cut high tax rates, the rich will consume more and invest more, and wealth will . . . . to the poor.
6. The government says that the property market is . . . . with laundered money from the drug cartels.
7. There is a constant . . . . of money in and out of the system.
8. We're . . . . as much money as we can into this project, millions in fact.
9. We've sunk millions of pounds into this factory. Its been a real . . . . on our resources.
10. We believe that the government should be . . . . more cash into education.
11. We have a liquidity problem; more money is . . . . out of the business than into it; in fact, we're haemorrhaging money.
12. When you look round their head offices, you get the impression that they're . . . . in cash.

EXERCISE 2

Complete the following. All the phrases have something to do with water. When you have filled in the gaps, underline the complete phrase.

crest	depth	under	fluid	sank	plug

1. You never hear about BNA. They . . . . without trace about 3 years ago.
2. Nobody knows whether the takeover is going ahead or not. The situation is very . . . . at the moment.
3. The banks have been riding on the . . . . of a wave for longer than anyone expected.
4. No wonder some of the smaller merchant banks have gone . . . . Some of them had no proper system of control.
5. They waited too long before they pulled the . . . . on that outfit in Singapore.
6. You're the derivatives expert. I'm totally out of my . . . . here.

Bankruptcy

EXERCISE 1

Choose the correct alternative to complete each sentence:

If a person or business has more debts than money to pay them, this means they have more
(1) . . . . than assets, and they are (2) . . . . If a (3) . . . . takes the matter to
court, the person or company is declared bankrupt. A bankrupt company goes into liquidation or
receivership or is wound up. The court appoints a liquidator (or receiver, or administrator) who realises
(ie sells) the company's (4) . . . . in order to repay creditors. A failing business can choose
voluntary winding up, in which case it appoints its own liquidator. In America a (5) . . . . in
difficulty can 'file for Chapter Eleven' and propose a recovery plan; it is then temporarily protected
from its creditors, and given some time to attempt to solve its problems. A failing business that
knows it has no reasonable chance of avoiding bankruptcy should stop trading. Continuing to
(6) . . . ., and building up debts with creditors that will never be paid, is called wrongful trading
and is illegal. There are limits to limited liability!

1.	a.	equity	b.	liability	c.	liabilities
2.	a.	illegal	b.	illiquid	c.	insolvent
3.	a.	borrower	b.	creditor	c.	debtor
4.	a.	assets	b.	debts	c.	liabilities
5.	a.	corporation	b.	partnership	c.	proprietor
6.	a.	do business	b.	earn	c.	make business

NOTE

In speech there are other more colourful, but less polite, ways of saying that a company has gone
bankrupt:

They've gone bust.	They've gone broke.	They've gone under.
They've gone to the wall.	They've gone belly up.	They've gone down the tubes.

EXERCISE 2

Complete the following sentences with either 'bankrupt' or 'bankruptcy'.

1.   The company has gone . . . .

2.   We're on the verge of . . . .

3.   If they keep spending money like that, they'll . . . . the company.

4.   I am sorry to say that we are facing . . . .

5.   There are limits to what an undischarged . . . . can do.

6.   We've got no choice but to declare ourselves . . . .

"Right, Mr Smith, just relax"

Phrasal Verbs – Bad Debts

EXERCISE 1

Match up the phrasal verbs on the left with the verbs that have a similar meaning on the right:

1.	bring about	a.	abandon debts as irrecoverable
2.	build up	b.	accumulate
3.	deal with a problem	c.	cause
4.	go under	d.	destroy
5.	plough back profits	e.	do something about a problem
6.	put up funds	f.	fail
7.	wind up	g.	force a company to stop trading
8.	wipe out	h.	provide funds
9.	write off	i.	re-invest profits

Which 2 of these verbs are regular?

Remember that the past form of the verb *wind, wound,* rhymes with *sound,* unlike the noun and verb *wound,* meaning an injury or to injure, in which the vowel rhymes with *soon.*

EXERCISE 2

Complete the text below using each of the phrasal verbs above once. You may need to use the past tense, the past participle or the present continuous form.

We had a serious problem with accounts receivable, and were forced to (1) . . . . thousands of pounds of bad debts, when one of our customers went bankrupt and was (2) . . . . by the receiver. If the managing director hadn't (3) . . . . some of his own money, the company could have been (4) . . . . For a time, it looked as if we were going to (5) . . . . We were teetering on the brink of bankruptcy. It became clear that we hadn't (6) . . . . enough of our earnings into the company, or (7) . . . . enough reserves to (8) . . . . such a situation. You often read about one bankruptcy (9) . . . . a chain of others – well, it nearly happened to us.

Auditing

EXERCISE 1

Number the following words or expressions with their <u>underlined</u> equivalents in the text:

accuracy (1)	**external**
Annual General Meeting	**implemented**
board of directors	**ratified**
checking	**shareholders (GB) or stockholders(US)**
deficiencies	**standard operating procedures**
determine	**subsidiaries**
deviations	**a synonym**
directives	**transnational corporations**

The traditional definition of auditing is a review and an evaluation of financial records by a second set of accountants. An internal audit is a control by a company's own accountants, checking for completeness, (1) <u>exactness</u> and reliability. Among other things, internal auditors are looking for (2) <u>departures</u> from (3) <u>a firm's established methods for recording business transactions.</u> In most countries, the law requires all firms to have their accounts audited by an outside company. An (4) <u>independent</u> audit is thus a review of financial statements and accounting records by an accountant not belonging to the firm. The auditors have to (5) <u>judge</u> whether the accounts give what in Britain is known as a "true and fair view" and in the US as a "fair presentation" of the company's [corporation's] financial position. Auditors are appointed by a company's (6) <u>most senior executives and advisors</u>, whose choice has to be (7) <u>approved</u> by the (8) <u>owners of the company's equity</u> at the (9) <u>company's yearly assembly.</u> Auditors write an official audit report. They may also address a "management letter" to the directors, outlining (10) <u>inadequacies</u> and recommending improved operating procedures. This leads to the more recent use of the word "audit" as (11) <u>an equivalent term</u> for "control": (12) <u>multinational companies,</u> for example, might undertake inventory, marketing and technical audits. Auditing in this sense means (13) <u>verifying</u> that general management (14) <u>instructions</u> are being (15) <u>executed</u> in branches, (16) <u>companies which they control,</u> etc.

EXERCISE 2

Add appropriate words to these phrases:

1. Auditors . . . . companies' accounts.

2. Accounts have to . . . . a fair presentation.

3. Auditors write a . . . .

4. It's the directors who . . . . the auditors.

5. Auditors sometimes . . . . better accounting procedures.

6. Using external auditors is a . . . . requirement.

Annual General Meetings

EXERCISE 1

Write the questions about AGMs to which these are the answers:

1. . . . .

   All the shareholders.

2. . . . .

   No, only the shareholders with voting shares. Sometimes there are categories of share that do not give their holder voting rights.

3. . . . .

   To approve (or reject) the company's accounts, and the auditors' and directors' reports of the year's activities; to elect (or re-elect) directors and auditors for the coming year; and to vote on the size of the dividend that will be paid.

4. . . . .

   The company generally sends them the Annual Report before they come to the meeting.

5. . . . .

   They can be represented by proxy; that means they can nominate someone else, called a proxy, to attend the meeting and vote for them.

6. . . . .

   There has to be a quorum – a minimum number of directors and shareholders present. The size of the quorum is usually specified in the company's Articles of Association, along with all the exact rules concerning shares, general meetings, the powers of directors, the election of officers, the approval of accounts, etc.

The following question starters may help you:

1. Who is eligible to . . . . ?
2. Are all the shareholders entitled to . . . . ?
3. What is the purpose of . . . . ?
4. What information . . . . ?
5. What happens if . . . . ?
6. How many shareholders . . . . ?

EXERCISE 2

Complete the following phrases:

1. The . . . . receive a copy of the . . . .
2. At the AGM, they have to . . . . the company's accounts.
3. They also . . . . the company's directors and . . . .
4. They vote on the size of the . . . . to be distributed.
5. Shareholders can appoint . . . . to vote in their place.

Cost Accounting

EXERCISE 1

The following sentences make up a short text about cost accounting. Decide which order they should go in:

a. But to this have to be added all the factory's overheads – rent or property taxes, electricity for lighting and heating, the price of the machine used, the maintenance department, the stores, the canteen, and so on.

b. Finally, where a company does not want to calculate the price of specific orders or processes, it can use full costing or absorption costing, which allocates all fixed and variable costs to the company's products.

c. For example, if you produce 500 wooden door-knobs, each one requiring 100 grams of wood and taking the machine operator two minutes to make, you can easily calculate the direct cost.

d. It is fairly easy to calculate the prime cost or direct cost of a manufactured article.

e. One of these is job-order cost accounting, which involves establishing a price for an individual item or a particular batch (a quantity of goods assembled or manufactured together).

f. There are also lots of other expenses of running a business that cannot be charged to any one product, process or department, and companies have to price their products in such a way as to cover their administration and selling expenses, the finance department, the research and development department, and so on.

g. This is the sum of the direct costs of the raw materials or components that make up the product and the labour required to produce it, which, of course, vary directly with production.

h. This is impossible where production involves a continuous process as with steel, flour, or cement. In this case companies often use process cost accounting, which determines costs over a given period of time.

i. Various methods can be used to allocate all these expenses to the selling price of different products.

1		2		3		4		5		6		7		8		9	

NOTE

British English *overheads* and *labour* = American English *overhead* and *labor*.

EXERCISE 2

Complete the following sentences:

1. Manufacturers have to find a way of . . . . all fixed and . . . . costs to their various products.

2. They have to cover the factory's . . . . , and things like administration and selling . . . .

3. The direct cost of . . . . and labour is easy to calculate.

Word Partnerships – Account

EXERCISE 1

All the words below can be combined with *account, accounts* or *accounting*, in a two-word partnership: e.g. *bank account, accounts payable* or *tax accounting*. Add the word *account, accounts* or *accounting* to each of the words below:

1. . . . . holder
2. . . . . methods
3. . . . . day
4. . . . . equation
5. . . . . payable
6. . . . . principles
7. . . . . period
8. . . . . procedures
9. . . . . receivable
10. . . . . standards
11. . . . . book

12. bank . . . .
13. current . . . .
14. deposit . . . .
15. cost . . . .
16. managerial . . . .
17. numbered . . . .
18. profit and loss . . . .
19. savings . . . .
20. tax . . . .

EXERCISE 2

Now complete the following sentences:

1. Auditors are supposed to make sure that companies follow their stated . . . .

2. Companies can choose from a variety of . . . . , but they are not allowed to change them too often.

3. Lots of money obtained in dubious or illegal ways is deposited in . . . . in Swiss banks.

4. The basic . . . . is Assets = Liabilities + Owners' Equity.

5. The . . . . at the London Stock Exchange usually lasts two weeks. It is followed by an . . . . on which all bills must be settled.

6. The . . . . is one of the three basic financial statements.

7. . . . . consist of money that is expected to be received. The contrary, ... , consist of money that is owed to other people.

8. The role of . . . . is to provide figures and statements that will aid decision-making.

Review – Accounting 1

EXERCISE 1

Classify the following 24 words into four groups of six, according to the headings below:

accounts payable	net profit	amortization	posting
annuity system	prudence	below the line	reducing balance
consistency	reserves	deferred liabilities	scrap value
double-entry	separate-entity	going-concern	straight line method
income statement	trial balance	journal	unit-of-measure
ledger	writing off	matching	voucher

Bookkeeping	**Accounting Principles**	**Depreciation**	**Financial Statements**
. . . .	. . . .	. . . .	. . . .
. . . .	. . . .	. . . .	. . . .
. . . .	. . . .	. . . .	. . . .
. . . .	. . . .	. . . .	. . . .
. . . .	. . . .	. . . .	. . . .
. . . .	. . . .	. . . .	. . . .

EXERCISE 2

Which of the words in Exercise 1 do the following sentences define?

1. . . . .

    A term to describe "extraordinary" items placed after the net profit total in a profit and loss account, which perhaps make the profit appear higher than it really is.

2. . . . .

    A way of depreciating an asset which involves estimating the number of years it will be used, and then dividing its historical cost by this number.

3. . . . .

    Money that a company will definitely have to repay in the future, but not during the current financial year.

4. . . . .

    The accounting principle that requires multinational companies to produce consolidated balance sheets in a single currency.

5. . . . .

    The accounting principle which assumes that a business will still be functioning next year and thereafter.

6. . . . .

    The American name for the entry on a balance sheet that shows how much money a business owes its suppliers for purchases made on credit.

7. . . . .

    The American name for what in Britain is usually called a profit and loss account.

8. . . . .

    The part of a company's profit that is retained for future reinvestment, rather than distributed as a dividend.

Review – Accounting 2

EXERCISE 1

In the wordbox below you should be able to find – horizontally (left to right), vertically (top to bottom), or diagonally (top left to bottom right) – at least 20 words used in accounting already seen in the previous pages.

D	C	R	E	D	I	T	F	A	I	R
A	D	O	W	E	N	R	L	C	N	E
T	S	E	W	B	P	U	O	C	C	V
A	O	S	B	I	A	E	W	R	O	E
B	J	Y	E	T	C	L	C	U	M	N
F	U	N	D	T	C	O	A	E	E	U
A	N	D	K	A	O	S	S	N	U	E
P	R	O	G	X	U	S	H	T	C	V
V	A	L	U	E	N	V	I	E	W	E
L	A	U	D	I	T	D	E	F	E	R

EXERCISE 2

Now complete the following sentences, using words from the wordbox above:

1. According to British law, a company's accounts have to give a . . . . of its financial situation.

2. An amount entered by a bookkeeper in the left-hand side of an account is a . . . .

3. I'm not going to spend the interest, but will let it . . . . in my bank account.

4. Since we can't afford it now, we are going to . . . . payment of this debt.

5. The amount of tax a company has to pay is included in the profit and loss . . . .

6. The firm's assets and liabilities are listed in the two columns of the . . . . sheet.

7. We've got half a dozen people from head office coming in next week, to . . . . the accounts.

8. We've worked out how much we expect to spend and to earn next year, and written it all down in the . . . .

Money and Banking

"If you owe your bank a hundred pounds, you have a problem.
If you owe it a million pounds, it has a problem!"

JOHN MAYNARD KEYNES

Forms of Money

Choose the correct alternative to complete each sentence:

1. Money in notes and coins is called
    a. cash   b. capital   c. reserves

2. The dollar, the mark and the yen are all
    a. currencies   b. funds   c. monies

3. Money borrowed from a bank is a
    a. deposit   b. income   c. loan

4. Borrowed money that has to be paid back constitutes a
    a. debt   b. fund   c. subsidy

5. All the money received by a person or a company is known as
    a. aid   b. income   c. wages

6. The money earned for a week's manual work is called
    a. income   b. salary   c. wages

7. The money paid for a month's (professional) work is a
    a. loan   b. salary   c. wages

8. Money placed in banks and other savings institutions constitutes
    a. capital   b. deposits   c. finance

9. Money paid by the government or a company to a retired person is a
    a. pension   b. rebate   c. subsidy

10. The money that will ultimately be used to pay pensions is kept in a
    a. budget   b. deposit   c. fund

11. The money needed to start a company is called
    a. aid   b. capital   c. debt

12. The money paid to lawyers, architects, private schools, etc. is called
    a. fees   b. instalments   c. wages

13. Regular part payments of debts are called
    a. deposits   b. loans   c. instalments

14. Part of a payment that is officially given back (for example, from taxes) is called a
    a. gift   b. instalment   c. rebate

15. Estimated expenditure and income is written in a
    a. budget   b. reserve   c. statement

16. A person's money in a business is known as his or her
    a. deposit   b. fund   c. stake

17. Money given to producers to allow them to sell cheaply is called a
    a. loan   b. rebate   c. subsidy

18. Money given to developing countries by richer ones is known as
    a. aid   b. debt   c. subsidy

Remember that *subvention* is not an English word.

Borrowing and Lending

Choose the correct alternative to complete each sentence:

1. If you possess something, you can say that you . . . . it.
    a. owe   b. own   c. owner

2. If you have to reimburse or repay someone, you . . . . money.
    a. owe   b. own   c. yield

3. To let someone else have the use of your money for a certain period of time, after which it must be paid back, is to . . . .
    a. borrow   b. lend   c. credit

4. To take money that has to be repaid is, on the contrary, to . . . .
    a. borrow   b. lend   c. steal

5. An amount of money lent is a . . . .
    a. debit   b. debt   c. loan

6. A person who has borrowed money is a . . . .
    a. creditor   b. debtor   c. owner

7. Another word for a lender is a/an . . . .
    a. creditor   b. debtor   c. owner

8. The income received by someone who lends money is called . . . .
    a. dividends   b. interest   c. interests

9. The borrower has to pay back the loan itself, also known as the . . . .
    a. principal   b. principle   c. premium

10. The amount of money a lender receives for a loan or an investment, expressed as a percentage, is known as its return or . . . .
    a. credit   b. income   c. yield

11. The following famous quotations are about credit and borrowing and lending. Can you complete them:
    a. In business, one way to obtain . . . . is to create the impression one already has it.
    b. Neither a . . . . nor a . . . . be.
    c. An acquaintance is someone we know well enough to . . . . from, but not well enough to . . . . to.
    d. A . . . . card is an anaesthetic which simply delays the pain.

Remember that *lend* is an irregular verb: *lend – lent – lent*

Central Banking

EXERCISE 1

Complete these sentences about Central Banks using the words in the box:

Central Banks, such as the Bank of England, the Federal Reserve Board in the US, and the Bundesbank in Germany:

act	control
fix	function
implement	influence
issue	supervise

1. . . . . as banks for the government and for other banks.

2. . . . . monetary policy - either the government's, as in Britain, or their own, if they are independent, as in Germany and the USA.

3. . . . . the money supply, measured by different aggregates such as M0, M1, M2, M3, etc.

4. . . . . the minimum interest rate.

5. . . . . as lender of last resort to commercial banks with liquidity problems.

6. . . . . coins and bank notes.

7. . . . . (floating) exchange rates by intervening in foreign exchange markets.

8. . . . . the banking system.

EXERCISE 2

Complete this paragraph using these words:

assets	cash	interest	liquid	maturity	reserve

Because a commercial bank can lend most of the money deposited with it to other borrowers, who in turn may lend it to another borrower, each sum of money deposited in a bank is multiplied several times. To ensure the safety of the banking system, central banks impose (1) . . . . requirements, obliging commercial banks to deposit a certain amount of money with the central bank at zero (2) . . . . Central banks in different countries also impose different "prudential ratios" on commercial banks. These are ratios between deposits and liquid (3) . . . . that are considered sufficient to meet demands for (4) . . . . (A bank's assets are its loans, which should, in theory, all be paid back one day, and its liabilities are the customers' deposits, which can all be withdrawn one day.) For example, a bank's capital ratio is between its capital and reserves on the one hand, and its total assets on the other. The reserve asset ratio is between deposits with a (5) . . . . of under two years, called "eligible liabilities," and reserve assets, which include cash and assets that are (6) . . . . – i.e. quickly convertible into cash – such as reserve deposits held by the central bank, and securities such as treasury bills.

The Money Supply

EXERCISE 1

Insert the words in the boxes in the following paragraphs:

bonds	**commercial**	**monetarist**
prices	**tight**	**velocity**

Following the (1) . . . . argument that the average level of (2) . . . . and wages is determined by the amount of money in circulation, and its (3) . . . . of circulation, many central banks now set money supply targets. By increasing or decreasing the money supply, the central bank indirectly influences interest rates, demand, output, growth, unemployment and prices. The central bank can reduce the reserves available to (4) . . . . banks by changing the reserve requirements. This reduces the amount of money that banks can create and makes money (5) . . . . or scarce. Alternatively, the central bank can engage in what are called open market operations, which involve selling short-term government (6) . . . . (such as three-month Treasury bills) to the commercial banks, or buying them back.

EXERCISE 2

Now do the same with this paragraph:

credit	**inflation**	**output**	**unemployment**
interest rates	**the exchange rate**		**aggregate demand**

When money is tight,

1. . . . . rise, because commercial banks have to borrow at a higher rate on the inter-bank market.

2. . . . . falls, because people and businesses borrow less at higher rates.

3. . . . . falls, because people and businesses buy less, as they have less money.

4. . . . . falls too, because with less consumption, firms produce less.

5. . . . . rises, because companies are producing and selling less, and so require less labour.

6. . . . . falls, because there is less money in circulation.

7. . . . . will probably rise, if there is the same demand but less money, or if there is higher demand, as foreigners take advantage of the higher interest rates to invest in the currency. Increasing the money supply, by making more reserves available, has the opposite effects.

Commercial Banking

Complete the text using these words:

accounts	**bank loan**	**cheque**	**customers'**
current account	**debt**	**depositors**	**deposits**
lend	**liabilities**	**liquidity**	**optimize**
overdraft	**salary**	**spread**	**standing orders**
return	**transfer**	**wages**	**withdraw**

Commercial banks are businesses that trade in money. They receive and hold (1) . . . . , pay money according to (2) . . . . instructions, (3) . . . . money, etc.

There are still many people in Britain who do not have bank (4) . . . . Traditionally, factory workers were paid (5) . . . . in cash on Fridays. Non-manual workers, however, usually receive a monthly (6) . . . . in the form of a cheque or a (7) . . . . paid directly into their bank account.

A (8) . . . . (US: checking account) usually pays little or no interest, but allows the holder to (9) . . . . his or her cash with no restrictions. Deposit accounts (in the US also called time or notice accounts) pay interest. They do not usually provide (10) . . . . (US: check) facilities, and notice is often required to withdraw money. (11) . . . . and direct debits are ways of paying regular bills at regular intervals.

Banks offer both loans and overdrafts. A (12) . . . . is a fixed sum of money, lent for a fixed period, on which interest is paid; banks usually require some form of security or guarantee before lending. An (13) . . . . is an arrangement by which a customer can overdraw an account, i.e. run up a debt to an agreed limit; interest on the (14) . . . . is calculated daily.

Banks make a profit from the (15) . . . . or differential between the interest rates they pay on deposits and those they charge on loans. They are also able to lend more money than they receive in deposits because (16) . . . . rarely withdraw all their money at the same time. In order to (17) . . . . the return on their assets (loans), bankers have to find a balance between yield and risk, and (18) . . . . and different maturities, and to match these with their (19) . . . . (deposits). The maturity of a loan is how long it will last; the yield of a loan is its annual (20) . . . . – how much money it pays – expressed as a percentage.

"Look – if you have five pocket calculators and I take two away, how many have you got left?"

Types of Bank

This exercise defines the most important kinds of bank. Complete the text using these words:

central banks	**building societies**	**finance house**
commercial banks	**merchant banks**	**investment banks**
supranational banks	**universal banks**	

(1) . . . . supervise the banking system; fix the minimum interest rate; issue bank notes; control the money supply; influence exchange rates; and act as lender of last resort.

(2) . . . . are businesses that trade in money. They receive and hold deposits in current and savings accounts, pay money according to customers' instructions, lend money, and offer investment advice, foreign exchange facilities, and so on. In some countries such as England these banks have branches in all major towns; in other countries there are smaller regional banks. Under American law, for example, banks can operate in only one state. Some countries have banks that were originally confined to a single industry, e.g. the Crédit Agricole in France, but these now usually have a far wider customer base.

In some European countries, notably Germany, Austria, and Switzerland, there are (3) . . . . which combine deposit and loan banking with share and bond dealing, investment advice, etc. Yet even universal banks usually form a subsidiary, known as a (4) . . . . , to lend money – at several per cent over the base lending rate – for hire purchase or instalment credit, that is, loans to consumers that are repaid in regular, equal monthly amounts.

In Britain, the USA and Japan, however, there is, or used to be, a strict separation between commercial banks and banks that do stockbroking or bond dealing. Thus in Britain, (5) . . . . specialise in raising funds for industry on the various financial markets, financing international trade, issuing and underwriting securities, dealing with takeovers and mergers, issuing government bonds, and so on.   They also offer stockbroking and portfolio management services to rich corporate and individual clients. (6) . . . . in the USA are similar, but they can only act as intermediaries offering advisory services, and do not offer loans themselves.

Yet despite the Glass-Steagall Act in the USA, and Article 65, imposed by the Americans in Japan in 1945, which enforce this separation, the distinction between commercial and merchant or investment banks has become less clear in recent years. Deregulation in the US and Britain is leading to the creation of "financial supermarkets" – conglomerates combining the services previously offered by stockbrokers, banks, insurance companies, etc.

In Britain there are also (7) . . . . that provide mortgages, i.e. they lend money to home-buyers on the security of houses and flats, and attract savers by paying higher interest than the banks. The savings and loan associations in the United States served a similar function, until most of them went spectacularly bankrupt at the end of the 1980s.

There are also (8) . . . . such as the World Bank or the European Bank for Reconstruction and Development, which are generally concerned with economic development.

Banking Products

Complete the text using these words:

cash dispensers	**cheque**	**credit card**
current account	**deposit account**	**foreign currency**
investment advice	**loan**	**mortgage**
overdraft	**pension**	**standing order**

My salary is paid directly into a low-interest (1) . . . . I can withdraw money from automatic (2) . . . . with a cashcard, so I hardly ever actually go into a bank. I pay regular, monthly bills by way of a (3) . . . . : the bank pays them according to my instructions, and debits my account. I pay irregular bills by (4) . . . . Nearly everyone I know in Britain has a chequebook, but when I lived on the Continent, I found that people hardly used them. They often paid cash, or paid bills at a post office with a paying-in slip.

I also have a (5) . . . . , which is useful for ordering things by post or on the telephone, and for travelling worldwide. I also use it in shops and restaurants, but try not to spend more than I can pay when the bill comes a month later, as this is a very expensive way of borrowing money. The annual interest is exorbitant – well over 20%.

I used to have a (6) . . . . in a building society which paid higher interest than the current account at the bank, but had restrictions as to how and when I could withdraw my money. But then we bought a flat. I got a 90% (7) . . . . from the building society: i.e. we had to pay a deposit of 10% with our own savings.

That is why I have no more money and no more deposit account. In fact I have arranged an (8) . . . . with the bank, which means I can occasionally withdraw more money than is actually in my account. Interest is calculated daily. Last year I asked the bank for a (9) . . . . to buy a car. I (only!) wanted two months salary, but they refused. Since I don't like the high interest rates that the garage's hire purchase people charge, I bought a cheap second-hand car instead.

I always use the bank to buy (10) . . . . when I go abroad, because their rates are better than the bureaux de change. I don't like travellers' cheques, and I've never had my money stolen – yet.

My bank is also always trying to sell me a private (11) . . . . plan, for when I retire, but I'm not interested. They also keep offering me (12) . . . . about shares, bonds, unit trusts, mutual funds, and so on. They don't seem to realize that if I could afford to buy all these things, I wouldn't need an overdraft.

Word Partnerships – Bank

EXERCISE 1

All the words below can be combined with *bank* or *banking* in a two-word partnership, e.g. *bank holiday* or *off-shore banking*. Add the word *bank* or *banking* either before or after each of the words below:

1. . . . . account . . . .
2. . . . . balance . . . .
3. . . . . central . . . .
4. . . . . clerk . . . .
5. . . . . commercial . . . .
6. . . . . deposit . . . .
7. . . . . holiday . . . .
8. . . . . investment . . . .
9. . . . . manager . . . .

10. . . . . merchant . . . .
11. . . . . note . . . .
12. . . . . off-shore . . . .
13. . . . . retail . . . .
14. . . . . robbery . . . .
15. . . . . savings . . . .
16. . . . . statement . . . .
17. . . . . system . . . .
18. . . . . wholesale . . . .

EXERCISE 2

Now complete the following sentences:

In my country the most important types of banks are:

. . . .

. . . .

The banking services that I use are:

. . . .

. . . .

"Congratulations, Mr Smith – as soon as I saw you I knew that you were the right man for the job"

Interest Rates

Choose words to complete each sentence. In some cases there is more than one possibility.

1. The Bank of England fixes a minimum interest rate, called the discount rate, at which it makes secured loans to . . . .

    a. big companies   b. private individuals   c. commercial banks   d. new businesses

2. British commercial banks lend to blue-chip borrowers (big, secure companies) at the . . . . The American equivalent is the prime rate.

    a. base rate   b. basic rate   c. discount rate   d. market rate

3. All other borrowers pay more, depending on the lender's estimation of their present and future solvency, also known as their creditworthiness or . . . . or . . . .

    a. credit   b. creditors   c. credit standing   d. credit rating

4. Borrowers can usually get a . . . . interest rate if the loan is guaranteed by securities or other collateral.

    a. higher   b. long-term   c. lower   d. riskier

5. Banks make their profits from the difference between the interest rate charged to borrowers and that paid to depositors, also known as a . . . . or . . . .

    a. margin   b. mistake   c. range   d. spread

6. Long-term interest rates are generally higher than short-term ones, except when the central bank temporarily reduces the money supply i.e. makes money . . . . or . . . .

    a. loose   b. scarce   c. tight   d. uncommon

7. These days many loans are made with . . . . or variable interest rates that change according to the supply and demand for money.

    a. drowning   b. floating   c. sinking   d. swimming

8. Borrowers and lenders can sometimes arrange limits beyond which rates cannot move. The upper limit is called a . . . . or a . . . .

    a. cap   b. ceiling   c. roof   d. summit

9. The lower limit on a variable rate loan is known as a . . . .

    a. bottom   b. carpet   c. floor   d. maturity

10. A . . . . is an arrangement that fixes both the upper and lower limits.

    a. collar   b. tie   c. shirt   d. suit

11. Central banks cannot determine the minimum lending rate for so-called Eurocurrencies – currencies held . . . .

    a. outside their country of origin   b. in Europe

12. Banks are able to offer better rates to borrowers of Eurocurrencies because there are no . . . . imposed by the central bank.

    a. discount rates   b. maturities   c. money supplies   d. reserve requirements

"Panic buying, I'm afraid – Cedric heard there was going to be a shortage."

Eurocurrencies

Sentences 1 to 10 make up a short text about Eurocurrencies. Complete each sentence, by taking a middle part from the second box and an end from the third box:

---

1. A Eurocurrency is any currency held
2. Thus Eurocurrencies do not necessarily
3. The Euromarket developed during the Cold War in the early 1950s,
4. This pool of dollars was later augmented by
5. The Euromarkets are still concentrated in London because
6. Since banks are not obliged to deposit any of their Eurocurrency assets
7. Therefore, international companies
8. Because the United States was, by definition,
9. Consequently in the early 1980s,
10. This succeeded in bringing

---

a. American trade deficits, and, after the 1974 and 1979 oil price rises,
b. at zero interest with the central bank,
c. have anything to do with Europe,
d. outside its country of origin,
e. some Eurodollar business
f. the American government allowed US banks special international banking facilities,
g. the one country that could not do Eurodollar business,
h. there are fewer governmental regulations there than in most other financial centres,
i. using US dollars for trade,
j. when the Russians, who were afraid that the Americans might freeze their dollar accounts in New York,

---

k. American banks were losing business.
l. and because the European time-zone is half-way between those of Japan and the USA.
m. back to New York City.
n. millions of "petrodollars" deposited by the newly-rich oil-producing countries.
o. often prefer to borrow Eurodollars.
p. so the name is not a very good one.
q. such as US$ in France, Yen in the US, or Deutschmarks in Japan.
r. they can give better interest rates (to both borrowers and depositors) than US-based banks.
s. transferred them to Europe, particularly to banks in London.
t. without reserve requirements and interest rate limits.

Sentence 1:	. . . .	. . . .	Sentence 6:	. . . .	. . . .
Sentence 2:	. . . .	. . . .	Sentence 7:	. . . .	. . . .
Sentence 3:	. . . .	. . . .	Sentence 8:	. . . .	. . . .
Sentence 4:	. . . .	. . . .	Sentence 9:	. . . .	. . . .
Sentence 5:	. . . .	. . . .	Sentence 10:	. . . .	. . . .

Exchange Rates

EXERCISE 1

Match the questions on the left with the responses on the right:

1. Is it true that there was a time when you could go to a bank in America and demand gold in exchange for your dollars?

   a. Because in reality, they are often determined by the massive amount of currency speculation that goes on. Currencies appreciate or depreciate for reasons that often have little to do with the countries' economic performance or international trade.

2. Who was he?

   b. "In God We Trust." Not "Gold"!

3. So they could never change?

   c. Not who, what. Or where. It was an international conference held in New Hampshire in 1944. It fixed the value of the US dollar at 1/35 of an ounce of gold, and "pegged" or fixed most other major currencies against the dollar.

4. But it's all different now?

   d. Oh sure, they can try to intervene on currency markets by buying or selling billions of dollars, or pounds, or whatever. But the speculators have much more money than governments.

5. No, what?

   e. Only if they were officially devalued or revalued by the government or the central bank.

6. So how does it work now?

   f. We have floating exchange rates, determined by supply and demand. Theoretically, the rates should reflect purchasing power parity – the cost of a given selection of goods and services in different countries.

7. Why "theoretically"?

   g. Well, in theory, yes. That was the result of Bretton Woods.

8. So there's nothing governments can do?

   h. Yes. The Bretton Woods system collapsed in the early 1970s because of inflation. There were too many dollars and not enough gold, so President Nixon ended gold convertibility. You know what it says on dollar bills now?

1	*g.*	2		3		4		5		6		7		8	

EXERCISE 2

Add appropriate words to these sentences:

1. Another verb for fixing exchange rates against something else is to . . . . them.
2. Increasing the value of an otherwise fixed exchange rate is called . . . .
3. Gold . . . . ended in the early 1970s.
4. The current system is one of . . . . exchange rates.
5. A currency can appreciate if lots of . . . . buy it.
6. In fact we have managed floating exchange rates, because governments and . . . . banks sometimes intervene on currency markets.

Third World Debt

EXERCISE 1

Rearrange the following sentences to make up a coherent and logical text about Third World debt. The first sentence is given to help you.

a. After the second oil shock of 1979, and the economic slowdown that followed it, interest rates rose and the prices of the commodities and agricultural goods exported by the debtor countries fell.

b. All this obviously makes most of the people in these countries much worse off than they were before their governments began borrowing to finance development.

c. Consequently they need to rollover or renew the loans, to reschedule or postpone repayments, or to borrow further money from the International Monetary Fund (IMF) just to pay the interest on existing loans from commercial banks.

d. For these reasons, many of the heavily indebted Third World countries are now unable to service their debts with Western commercial banks: i.e., they cannot pay the interest, let alone repay the principal.

e. In many countries, this worked successfully for a few years, but after the huge rise in oil prices in 1973, while the oil-exporting nations were depositing their "petrodollars" in Western banks, many developing countries needed to borrow more money to pay for their imported oil.

f. In the 1960s, many developing countries with low productivity, low income, and low saving rates began to borrow large sums of money from Western banks, in order to industrialize.

g. In the 1990s, while much of the Third World was paying billions of dollars of interest to the IMF (but hardly reducing the size of the loans themselves), the commercial banks started to lend billions of dollars to the former "Second World" – the previously communist countries of Eastern and Central Europe.

h. In these circumstances, when rescuing or "bailing out" indebted countries, the IMF insists on "structural adjustment" and "austerity" measures, obliging governments to devalue, to privatize as much as possible, to cut spending on health care, education and transport, to end food subsidies, and to export everything that can be sold, including food.

i. In the late 1980s, many Western banks and governments (but not the IMF) began to write off or cancel a proportion of the loans made to Third World countries which had defaulted, although the proportion cancelled is generally less than the amount that the countries were repaying anyway.

1	*f.*	2		3		4		5		6		7		8		9	

EXERCISE 2

Now complete the following sentences:

1. If you borrow money you have to pay ....

2. When the loan matures you have to pay back the ....

3. Many developing countries are now heavily ....

4. To service a debt is to ....

5. To default on a debt is to ....

6. To bail someone out is to ....

7. To rollover a debt is to ....

8. To reschedule a debt is to ....

9. To write off a debt is to ....

Banking Verbs

Across

1. "Of course I don't have that kind of money. I had to . . . . it ." (6)

4. See 10 across.

5. "I showed the bank my business plan, and they offered to . . . . me everything I asked for." (4)

7. With the cheque guarantee card, shops know that the bank will . . . . any cheque up to £100. (6)

9. "When I discovered my mistake, I immediately called the bank and asked them to . . . . the cheque." (4)

10. and 4. The borrower was unable to repay the principal, and asked the bank to . . . . the loan. (4, 4)

12. "I had to stand in a queue for fifteen minutes just to . . . . a five pound cheque." (4)

13. and 18. down. An important function of a central bank is to act as lender of . . . . (4, 6)

16. "We nearly went bust, but at the last minute the bank agreed to . . . . us out." (4)

19. "When I pointed out to the bank that it was their mistake, they agreed to . . . . me all the extra charges I'd paid." (9)

21. See 22 across.

22. and 21. When it becomes obvious that it has a bad debt, the bank has to . . . . it . . . . (5, 3)

23. Investment banks usually . . . . in stocks and bonds. (5)

24. An investment with a high risk is usually compensated by way of a high . . . . (5)

Down

2. "I can't borrow any more; I already . . . . the bank over £10,000." (3)

3. "This wonderful piece of plastic allows me to . . . . cash all over Europe!" (8)

4. "With all that money you got for your birthday you should go and . . . . a savings account." (4)

6. "Did you know that they even have machines now where you can . . . . as well as take out money?" (7)

8. Since they clearly couldn't afford to pay back the loans then, the banks had to agree to . . . . .the debt. (10)

9. The clearing system makes it much easier to . . . . inter-bank debts. (6)

11. "They agreed to grant me a . . . . for six months." (4)

14. "If they make another big mistake like that I'm going to . . . . all my connections with that bank." (5)

15. It is usually the role of the central bank to . . . . the minimum interest rate. (3)

17. Many Third World countries are unable to . . . . their debts, let alone repay the principal. (7)

18. See 13 across.

20. Companies generally use investment banks to . . . . new shares or bonds for them. (5)

Banking Services

Add the words and expressions that complete the following sentences to the wordbox below:

1. When I opened the account, they gave me a . . . . (10) and a paying-in book.

2. Banks' basic business used to be making . . . . (5), but they now often earn more from securities trading and financial services.

3. Most banks are able to offer . . . . (10,6) to rich clients.

4. An importer who has to pay a bill in a foreign currency, and so cannot use a cheque, can arrange to pay by . . . . (7,5).

5. Outside banking hours, shops and other businesses can deposit money in the bank's . . . . (5,4).

6. Before travelling abroad, I always get some currency from the . . . . (7,8) department of the bank.

7. I pay regular bills every month with a . . . . (8,5).

8. My salary is paid directly into my account every month by an automatic . . . . (8).

9. Nearly all restaurants accept payment by . . . . (6,4).

10. Most people in Britain who buy a house take out a . . . . (8).

11. Since I sometimes spend more than I have in my current account, I have arranged an . . . . (9).

12. If you want higher interest, and don't need to withdraw money too often, you should get a . . . . (7,7).

13. A . . . . (6,2,6) is a paper issued by a buyer's bank which guarantees that the seller will be paid.

14. If you want to write cheques and have easy access to your money at any time, you should have a . . . . (7,7).

15. People with valuables often keep them in a . . . . (4,7, 3) in a bank.

1. ▢▢▢▢▢ **B** ▢▢▢
2. ▢ **A** ▢
3. ▢▢▢▢ **N** ▢▢▢▢▢
4. ▢ **K** ▢▢▢
5. **I**
6. ▢▢ **N** ▢▢
7. ▢ **G** ▢▢
8. ▢ **S** ▢
9. ▢ **E** ▢▢▢
10. ▢ **R**
11. ▢ **V**
12. ▢▢ **I** ▢
13. ▢▢▢ **C** ▢▢
14. ▢▢ **E** ▢▢▢
15. ▢▢▢ **S** ▢▢▢

Insurance

Number the following words with their <u>underlined</u> equivalents in the text:

affluent	**catastrophes**	**claims**
commission	**gilts**	**huge**
indemnify	**insurance brokers**	**policy**
retires	**sums**	**underwritten**

Insurance is designed to provide a sum of money to compensate for any damage suffered as the result of a risk that has been insured against in a specific insurance (1) <u>contract,</u> such as fire, accident, theft, loss, damage, injury or death. Thousands of people pay premiums to insurance companies, which use the money to (2) <u>compensate</u> people who suffer loss or damage, etc. Some people also use insurance policies as a way of saving. Life assurance policies, for example, usually pay a certain sum on a specific date – for example, when a person (3) <u>stops working at the age of 60 or 65 or whenever</u>, or earlier if the person dies.

Insurance companies, like pension funds, are large institutional investors that place great (4) <u>amounts</u> of money in various securities: shares, bonds, (5) <u>British government bonds</u>, etc.

Insurance companies generally employ their own agents who sell insurance to customers, but there are also (6) <u>other middlemen</u> who work with several companies, selling insurance in return for a (7) <u>percentage of the premium</u>.

If a particular insurance company considers that the risk it has (8) <u>assumed responsibility for</u> is too big, it might share the business with other companies, by way of reinsurance. Lloyds of London underwrites a great many risks which are spread among lots of syndicates, made up of groups of (9) <u>wealthy</u> people known as "names." In return for earning a percentage of the insurance premiums, the names have unlimited liability for losses. After a series of (10) <u>demands for payment</u> following lots of (11) <u>natural disasters</u> (shipwrecks, earthquakes, hurricanes, and so on) in the late 1980s, many Lloyds syndicates had to make (12) <u>enormous</u> pay-outs, and many names were bankrupted.

"What do you mean you've resigned?"

Time Metaphors

There are a lot of common metaphorical expressions in English which reveal that we think of time as a limited resource or a valuable commodity.

We often talk about spending, investing, saving, wasting, and using up time, of having enough time left, or running out of time, of giving somebody your time, of something taking up too much time, of having no time to spare or to lose, of something not being worth our time, and so on.

Complete the sentences below using the correct form of the following words:

save	**lose**	**give**	**run**	**waste (x2)**	**spend**
left	**worth**	**spare**	**take (x2)**	**invest**	**allocate**

1. I need a decision fast. We're . . . . out of time.

2. How much time do we have . . . . ?

3. It's a complete . . . . of time.

4. Stop . . . . my time!

5. It'll . . . . time if we all get a copy of the figures before the meeting.

6. I'd like to help you but I'm so busy, I just can't . . . . the time.

7. I'm not sure this project is . . . . the time it's going to take to get it off the ground.

8. Look, we've . . . . a great deal of time and effort in this. We can't back out now.

9. We need to do something about it straightaway. There's no time to . . . .

10. We obviously need to . . . . more time for the preliminary study before we take this any further.

11. Why isn't your report finished? You've been . . . . more than enough time to do it.

12. We had to . . . . a lot of time getting to know the Saudis before we could get down to negotiations.

13. Don't worry. Everything will work out fine. It's just going to . . . . a little more time than we expected, that's all.

14. No, you can't have another week to work on it. This has . . . . up far too much time already.

Trade and Commerce

"Under capitalism man exploits man. Under socialism
it's just the opposite."
ANON.

Ways of Selling 1

Match the words in the box with the definitions below:

agent	**broker**	**consumer**	**customer**
distributor	**franchisee**	**merchant**	**middlemen**
outlet	**sales force**	**retailer**	**wholesaler**

1. . . . . : an agent in a particular market, such as securities, commodities, insurance, etc.

2. . . . . : a general term for agents, brokers, dealers, merchants, traders, wholesalers, retailers, and other marketing intermediaries.

3. . . . . : a merchant such as a shopkeeper who sells to the final customer.

4. . . . . : a place where goods are sold to the public – a shop, store, kiosk, market stall, etc.

5. . . . . : a collective term for a company's sales representatives or commercial travellers
GB *Sales representatives, commercial travellers* = US *salespersons, traveling salesmen.*

6. . . . . : an intermediary who stocks goods from various suppliers and delivers them to retailers when ordered.

7. . . . . : a person (generally a wholesaler) who stocks and resells components or goods to manufacturers or retailers.

8. . . . . : a person (or company) who buys a product or service from a producer or a shop.

9. . . . . : a person who buys (and takes possession of) goods, and sells them on his or her own account.

10. . . . . : a person who buys an exclusive right to sell certain products in a certain area (or to use a particular name).

11. . . . . : a person who negotiates purchases and sales in return for commission or a fee.

12. . . . . : the end-user of goods or services, whose needs are satisfied by producers.

Ways of Selling 2

EXERCISE 1

Complete the text by inserting the following words in the gaps:

agent	**authorized dealer**	**chain**	**end-users**
franchise	**industrial**	**outlet**	**premises**
retailer	**sales reps**	**telephone**	**vending machines**

Very few producers make their goods and sell them directly to their (1) . . . . from the same
(2) . . . . There are usually specialized marketing intermediaries involved in getting goods
or services to the right place – a sales (3) . . . . convenient to consumers – at the right time.
These intermediaries constitute a distribution channel or a (4) . . . . of distribution.

The shortest channel exists in cases of direct marketing, where the manufacturer sells direct to
consumers, reaching them by (5) . . . . or direct mail, or by way of its own (6) . . . .,
who contact existing and potential customers, and try to persuade them to buy goods or services. More
common are channels with a single intermediary – e.g. a sales agent or broker for (7) . . . .
goods, a (8) . . . . for consumer goods, an (9) . . . . in the automobile industry, or a
(10) . . . . in the fashion, car hire and fast-food businesses. More complex channels add further
intermediaries such as wholesalers, and where goods are exported, very likely an (11) . . . . as
well.

Marketing channels change over time. For example, in retailing, the development of department
stores, chain stores, mail order firms, supermarkets, (12) . . . ., hypermarkets on the edge of
town, franchising systems, and so on, are all twentieth century developments. The twenty-first century
promises virtual reality shopping.

EXERCISE 2

**Here are six popular quotations about the world of selling. Match up the two halves to make the
quotations:**

1. When buyers don't fall for prices,   a.   prices must fall for buyers.

2. Pile it high   b.   and everything is marketing.

3. It is not enough to succeed;   c.   and sell it cheap.

4. A man without a smiling face   d.   others must fail.

5. Marketing is everything   e.   then what were we buying before?

6. If every new product is 'improved'   f.   must not open a shop.

1		2		3		4		5		6	

Do you have any favourite quotations?

International Trade

Replace the underlined words and expressions in the text with the words and expressions in the box:

balance of payments	**balance of trade**	**barter** or **counter-trade**
climate	**commodities**	**division of labour**
economies of scale	**factors of production**	**nations**
protectionism	**quotas**	**tariffs**

(1) <u>Countries</u> import some goods and services from abroad, and export others to the rest of the world. Trade in (2) <u>raw materials and goods</u> is called visible trade in Britain and merchandise trade in the US. Services, such as banking, insurance, tourism, and technical expertise, are invisible imports and exports. A country can have a surplus or a deficit in its (3) <u>difference between total earnings from visible exports and total expenditure on visible imports</u>, and in its (4) <u>difference between total earnings from all exports and total expenditure on all imports</u>. Most countries have to pay their deficits with foreign currencies from their reserves, although of course the USA can usually pay in dollars, the unofficial world trading currency. Countries without currency reserves can attempt to do international trade by way of (5) <u>direct exchanges of goods without the use of money</u>. The (imaginary) situation in which a country is completely self-sufficient and has no foreign trade is called autarky.

The General Agreement on Tariffs and Trade (GATT), concluded in 1994, aims to maximize international trade and to minimize (6) <u>the favouring of domestic industries</u>. GATT is based on the comparative cost principle, which is that all nations will raise their income if they specialize in producing the commodities in which they have the highest relative productivity. Countries may have an absolute or a comparative advantage in producing particular goods or services, because of (7) <u>inputs</u> (raw materials, cheap or skilled labour, capital, etc.), (8) <u>weather conditions</u>, (9) <u>specialization of work into different jobs</u>, (10) <u>savings in unit costs arising from large-scale production</u>, and so forth. Yet most governments still pursue protectionist policies, establishing trade barriers such as (11) <u>taxes charged on imports</u>, (12) <u>restrictions on the quantity of imports</u>, administrative difficulties, and so on.

Does your country have a trade surplus or deficit?
Does it have a balance of payments surplus or deficit?
What are its chief exports?
Which industries or sectors are protected?
Which do you think should be protected?

Imports and Exports

EXERCISE 1

This exercise concerns methods of payment used in international trade.
Match the first half of the sentence on the left with the second half on the right:

1. A pro-forma invoice is the first draft of an exporter's bill to an importer

2. A commercial bill or a bill of exchange is a written order instructing someone

3. The opposite is a letter of credit – a paper issued by a buyer's bank as proof that the seller will be paid;

4. Exporters can also sell their bills of exchange, at a discount,

5. A bill of lading is a document giving title to goods that acts as a receipt and a contract to ship them;

6. Most industrialized countries, eager to increase their exports, have government agencies

7. Some countries go even further,

8. A company short of liquidity and with a lot of "receivables" can sell them at a discount

a. (usually an importer) to pay someone else (usually an exporter) a certain sum on a given date.

b. containing estimated prices, according to which the importer will decide whether to buy or not.

c. giving loans to developing countries so that they can (eventually) buy their exports.

d. shippers can use them as security when discounting bills of exchange.

e. that either give loans to exporters awaiting payment or guarantee exporters against bad debts.

f. the seller can then sell the letter (at a discount) on the commercial paper market.

g. to accepting houses or other merchant banks (if the bank believes that the debtor will pay up).

h. to someone who will try to collect the debt (at full value); this is known as factoring.

1	2	3	4	5	6	7	8

EXERCISE 2

Add appropriate words to these sentences:

1. Selling a bill or a financial instrument at a . . . . means selling it at less than 100%.
2. Letters of credit can be . . . . like other financial assets.
3. An accepting house is a specialized . . . . bank.
4. A bill of . . . . proves the ownership of goods.
5. Factoring is a way of trading . . . .

Incoterms

In international trade, prices are often quoted in "Incoterms" such as those in this exercise. These are internationally accepted expressions for foreign trade contracts, established by the International Chamber of Commerce in Paris.

Match the first half of the sentence on the left with the second half on the right:

1. "Ex-works" refers to the cost of the goods at the suppliers' factory gate;

   a. cost and freight, but not insurance, to this port of destination.

2. "Ex-warehouse" means much the same thing except that

   b. for goods delivered duty paid to the buyer's premises in Geneva.

3. "FAS Rotterdam" is the abbreviation for "free alongside ship, Rotterdam" – this price includes

   c. from the port to the named destination: not all importers are in towns with sea-ports!

4. "FOB Liverpool" means "free on board, Liverpool"; in other words the seller's price

   d. imports are usually priced CIF and exports FOB, as transport is generally paid by the purchaser.

5. "C&F Hamburg" is the price covering

   e. in other words, the price of goods and transport (but not insurance) to a named destination.

6. "CIF New York" is the price covering

   f. includes all charges up to and including loading the goods onto a ship.

7. "CIP Paris" is short for "carriage, insurance paid", and includes the price of transport by container

   g. the cost of the goods, insurance, and freight to this destination port.

8. "DCP" stands for "delivered carriage paid",

   h. the warehouse could belong to a wholesaler, distributor or exporter rather than a manufacturer.

9. "DDP Geneva" would be an inclusive price

   i. transport as far as the port; the buyer pays for loading onto the ship, shipping, and insurance.

10. For the purposes of calculating trade figures,

   j. i.e., the buyer or importer pays for freight (or carriage or transport) and insurance.

1		2		3		4		5		6		7		8		9		10	

Financing Foreign Trade

EXERCISE 1

One way of financing international trade is by a letter of credit. The foreign buyer transfers money from its bank to a correspondent bank in the exporter's country. This bank then informs the exporter that a letter of credit for a sum of money is available when it presents a bill of lading (a document prepared by the shipowner or his agent which acknowledges that the goods have been received on board the ship), a commercial invoice, and an insurance certificate.

Another possibility is to pay by a bill of exchange, as in the following example of the export of a shipment of goods from Britain to Argentina.

What is the correct order of the following paragraphs?

a. Meanwhile, the British manufacturer can sell the bill of exchange (at a discount) to an accepting house in London, so that it does not have to wait for payment.
b. On receiving an order from Argentina, a British manufacturer produces the goods. After arranging insurance, the manufacturer will send the goods to the port, with an invoice and a bill of lading, to be loaded onto a ship. When the goods have been shipped on board, the ship's master signs and returns the bill of lading to the producer.
c. On the agreed date, the importer honours the bill of exchange.
d. The exporter will draw up a bill of exchange requiring the buyer to pay a certain sum of money on an agreed date, and present the bill to a London correspondent bank of the buyer's bank.
e. The London bank accepts a bill of exchange for the same amount. It will then send the bill of lading and the bill of exchange to Argentina.
f. When the documents arrive in Argentina, they will be given to the importing company when it accepts the original bill of exchange.
g. When the ship reaches its destination, the importer presents the documents to the master of the ship, and collects the goods. (If the goods do not arrive, the buyer will have to make an insurance claim.)

1	*b.*	2		3		4		5		6		7	

EXERCISE 2

1. Find *five* verbs in the text that partner the noun *goods*.

....

2. Find *six* verbs in the text that partner the noun *bill of exchange*.

....

3. Find *five* different financial documents mentioned above.

....

Pricing

Read the following text and then decide whether the statements on the next page are TRUE or FALSE:

Companies' pricing decisions depend on one or more of three basic factors: production and distribution costs, the level of demand, and the prices (or probable prices) of current and potential competitors. Companies also consider their overall objectives and their consequent profit or sales targets, such as seeking maximum revenue, or maximum market share, etc. Pricing strategy must also consider market positioning: quality products generally require "prestige pricing" and will probably not sell if their price is thought to be too low.

Obviously, firms with excess production capacity, a large inventory, or a falling market share, tend to cut prices. Firms experiencing cost inflation, or in urgent need of cash, tend to raise prices. A company faced with demand that exceeds its possibility to supply is also likely to raise its prices.

When sales respond directly to price variations, demand is said to be elastic. If sales remain stable after a change in price, demand is inelastic. Although it is an elementary law of economics that the lower the price, the greater the sales, there are numerous exceptions. For example, price cuts can have unpredictable psychological effects: buyers may believe that the product is faulty or of lower quality, or will soon be replaced, or that the firm is going bankrupt, etc. Similarly, price rises convince some customers that the product must be of high quality, or will soon become very hard to get hold of, and so on!

A psychological effect that many retailers count on is that a potential customer seeing a price of £499 will register the £400 price range rather than the £500. This technique is known as "odd pricing".

Obviously most customers consider elements other than price when buying something: the "total cost" of a product can include operating and servicing costs, and so on. Since price is only one element of the marketing mix, a company can respond to a competitor's price cut by modifying other elements: improving its product, service, communications, etc. Reciprocal price cuts may only lead to a price war, good for customers but disastrous for producers who merely end up losing money.

Whatever pricing strategies a marketing department selects, a product's selling price generally represents its total cost (unit cost plus overheads) plus profit or "risk reward". Overheads are the various expenses of operating a plant that cannot be charged to any one product, process or department, which have to be added to prime cost or direct cost which covers material and labour. Cost accountants have to decide how to allocate or assign fixed and variable costs to individual products, processes or departments.

Microeconomists argue that in a fully competitive industry, price equals marginal cost equals minimum average cost equals breakeven point (including a competitive return on capital), and that a company's maximum-profit equilibrium is where extra costs are balanced by extra revenue, in other words, where the marginal cost curve intersects the marginal revenue curve. In reality, many companies have little idea what their optimal price or production volume is, while most microeconomists are happier with their models than actually talking to production managers, marketers or cost accountants!

EXERCISE 1

1. There are three basic factors potentially involved in all pricing decisions.   TRUE/FALSE

2. When pricing a product, companies have to think of potential as well as existing competitors.   TRUE/FALSE

3. You are unlikely to sell high quality products at a low price.   TRUE/FALSE

4. When demand exceeds supply, a company nearly always increases its prices.   TRUE/FALSE

5. A company faced with rising costs has to increase its prices.   TRUE/FALSE

6. A company can only change a price if it is "inelastic".   TRUE/FALSE

7. Pricing is often strongly influenced by psychological factors.   TRUE/FALSE

8. A company can respond to competitors' price cuts by changing different elements of the marketing mix.   TRUE/FALSE

9. Prices generally take into account both direct and indirect costs.   TRUE/FALSE

10. In theory, a product's price should equal its marginal cost and the company's breakeven point.   TRUE/FALSE

EXERCISE 2

Now complete the following word partnerships from the text:

1. breakeven . . . .

2. . . . . capacity

3. distribution . . . .

4. . . . . targets

5. . . . . positioning

6. . . . . share

7. odd . . . .

8. prime . . . .

9. . . . . accountant

10. variable . . . .

"At the moment Mr Grilph is in one of those periods between losing and making fortunes.

EXERCISE 3

Which of these three summaries most fully and accurately expresses the main ideas of the text on pricing?

First summary

The prices companies charge for their products depend on many factors: their costs, the level of demand, competitors' prices, financial targets, marketing strategies, market positioning, production capacity, inventory size, inflation, and so on. Yet pricing strategies are often unsuccessful because of the unpredictable psychological reactions of customers. Consequently companies often concentrate instead on other elements of the marketing mix: product improvement, service, communications, etc. Even so, companies have to make sure they cover direct costs and overheads. This usually results in a price that equals both marginal cost and breakeven point.

Second summary

The most important factors in pricing decisions are production costs (including overheads), the level of demand, and the going market price. Yet broader company objectives, and profit or sales targets, and market positioning, are also important. There are also lots of circumstances that might cause companies to change their prices: excess production capacity, large inventories, or a falling market share on the one hand, or cost inflation, an urgent need for cash, or demand that exceeds supply, on the other. Yet perfectly logical decisions regarding prices thought to be elastic can have unpredictable psychological effects. It is also clear that customers are influenced by elements other than price, so companies can equally modify other elements of the marketing mix. In a competitive industry, price is generally not much greater than marginal cost and breakeven point.

Third summary

Companies' pricing decisions generally depend on factors such as production and distribution costs, consumer demand, and competitors' prices. Yet a company's overall objectives and profit or sales targets are also important. Of course there are situations in which a company will raise its prices (e.g. excess production capacity, a large inventory, or a falling market share) or lower them (e.g. excessive demand, cost inflation, a cash shortage). In general, the lower the price, the greater the sales. Companies take account of psychological effects and use techniques such as odd pricing. Companies can also change other elements of the marketing mix, especially if this allows them to avoid a damaging price war. Whatever happens, companies generally have to cover a product's total cost and make a profit. This is difficult in a competitive industry, as here price will only equal breakeven point.

Pricing Strategies

Match up the remarks below with the names of different pricing strategies in the box:

---

1. market penetration pricing
2. market skimming
3. current-revenue pricing
4. loss-leader pricing
5. mark-up or cost-plus pricing
6. going-rate pricing
7. demand-differential pricing (or price discrimination)
8. perceived-value pricing

---

a. Firstly we need cash, and secondly, we don't think the product will last very long – it's really just a gimmick – so we're trying to maximize our sales income now.

b. Like all supermarkets, we offer half a dozen or more different items at a really low price each week. We lose on those, but customers come in and buy lots of other stuff as well.

c. Since our product is indistinguishable from those of all our competitors, and we've only got a tiny part of the market, we charge the same as the rest of them.

d. They just worked out the unit cost and added a percentage, without even considering demand elasticity or anything like that.

e. We charge an extremely high price because we know people will pay it. Our brand name is so famous for quality – we can make huge profits.

f. We charge lots of different prices for what is really almost the same thing. Of course, in First Class you get better food, and in Economy there's hardly any legroom, but it's still a flight from A to B.

g. We decided to launch the product at a very low price, almost at direct cost, hoping to get a big market share. Then we can make profits later because of economies of scale.

h. We're going to charge a really high price to start with. We can always lower it later to reach price-elastic market segments.

1		2		3		4		5		6		7		8	

Word Partnerships – Price

EXERCISE 1

All the words below can be combined with *price* in a two-word partnership: e.g. *price war, retail price*. Add the word *price* either before or after each of the words below:

1. .... control	14. .... market ....
2. .... cost	15. .... mechanism ....
3. .... cut	16. .... minimum ....
4. .... discrimination	17. .... range ....
5. .... elasticity	18. .... recommended ....
6. .... exercise	19. .... reduction ....
7. .... fixing	20. .... retail ....
8. .... freeze	21. .... rise ....
9. .... going	22. .... selling ....
10. .... historical	23. .... sensitivity ....
11. .... index	24. .... strike ....
12. .... list	25. .... war ....
13. .... maintenance	26. .... wholesale ....

EXERCISE 2

Which of these two-word nouns refers to:

1. a basic price before discounts and special offers are made?
2. aggressive competition between rivals?
3. a price at which retailers buy goods?
4. a price recorded in a company's accounts?
5. the government's measure of inflation?
6. the price at which a producer makes no profit?
7. the relationship between a product's price and the quantity bought?

Which two of these two-word nouns refer to:

8. a price-limit imposed by the government?
9. arrangements between competitors not to lower prices?
10. the price of options?

Word Partnerships – Cost

EXERCISE 1

All the words below can be combined with *cost* in a two-word partnership, e.g. *cost accounting*, *variable cost*. Add the word *cost* either before or after each of the words below.

1. . . . . accounting	11. . . . . labour . . . .
2. . . . . advantage	12. . . . . leadership . . . .
3. . . . . average	13. . . . . marginal . . . .
4. . . . . carrying	14. . . . . opportunity . . . .
5. . . . . current	15. . . . . price . . . .
6. . . . . direct	16. . . . . prime . . . .
7. . . . . factory	17. . . . . replacement . . . .
8. . . . . fixed	18. . . . . total . . . .
9. . . . . historical	19. . . . . unit . . . .
10. . . . . indirect	20. . . . . variable . . . .

EXERCISE 2

Complete the following sentences using two-word partnerships from the list above.

1. Companies' balance sheets usually record assets at . . . .

2. They don't record the . . . . because they usually don't know it.

3. Prime cost and . . . . mean the same thing: the cost of raw materials and labour.

4. . . . . – such as rent and salaries – do not vary according to the volume a company produces.

5. . . . ., on the contrary, are those which depend on the volume of output produced.

6. Dumping means selling goods at below . . . .

7. Some companies employ a . . . . strategy – aimed at producing goods at a lower cost than their competitors.

8. Economists define . . . . as the additional cost of producing one more unit of a product.

9. . . . . is the amount that a factor of production (land, labour, or capital) could have earned if put to another use.

10. . . . . is the cost of owning assets, which can be compared with the amount of interest that could be earned if the money was lent instead.

Review – Trade and Commerce

Add the words that complete the following sentences to the wordbox below:

1. A collective word for all the places where a company's goods are sold is . . . . (7).
2. Many producers use an independent . . . . (11) to get their goods to retailers.
3. Exporters are often paid by way of a bill of . . . . (8).
4. Another name for a consumer is an . . . . (3-4).
5. A . . . . (10) is an intermediary who stocks goods and delivers them to retailers.
6. If you can increase profits by selling more goods at a lower price, their price can be described as . . . . (7).
7. The intermediaries involved in moving goods from the producer to the customer make up a distribution . . . . (7).
8. Another word for the intermediaries between producer and customer is . . . . (9).
9. The price of labour and materials determines a product's . . . . (6, 4)
10. The person who uses something is called a consumer; the person who buys something in a store is a . . . . (8).
11. The export of services is good for a country's balance of . . . . (8).
12. Charging a high price for a new product is known as market . . . . (8).
13. As well as labour and materials (and profit), the price of a product also covers the manufacturer's . . . . (9).
14. Apart from inside customs unions like the EU and NAFTA, goods imported from abroad are generally subject to . . . . (7).
15. Agents often deal in goods they do not actually possess; someone who takes possession of goods before selling them is called a . . . . (8).
16. Selling a new product cheaply in order to get a large market share is called market . . . . (11).

			1.			**T**							
2.						**R**							
3.						**A**							
			4.			**D**							
5.						**E**							
			6.			**A**							
		7.				**N**							
		8.				**D**							
9.						**C**							
10.						**O**							
	11.					**M**							
	12.					**M**							
		13.				**E**							
		14.				**R**							
15.						**C**							
16.						**E**							

Company Finance

"Pan Am takes good care of you. Marks and Spencer love you,
Securicor cares. At Amstrad, we want your money."

ALAN SUGAR (founder of Amstrad)

Stocks and Shares 1

EXERCISE 1

Read the following text and then decide whether the statements following are TRUE or FALSE:

The act of issuing shares (GB) or stocks (US) – i.e. offering them for sale to the public – for the first time, is known as floating a company or making a flotation. Companies generally use a bank to underwrite the issue. In return for a fee, the bank guarantees to purchase the security issue at an agreed price on a certain day, although it hopes to sell it to the public. Newer and smaller companies trade on "over-the-counter" markets, such as the Unlisted Securities Market in London. Successful companies can apply to have their shares traded on the major stock exchanges, but in order to be quoted (GB) or listed (US) there, they have to fulfil a large number of requirements. One of these is to send their shareholders independently-audited annual reports, including the year's trading results and a statement of the company's financial position.

Buying a share gives its holder part of the ownership of a company. Shares generally entitle their owners to vote at companies' General Meetings, to elect company directors, and to receive a proportion of distributed profits in the form of a dividend (or to receive part of the company's residual value if it goes into bankruptcy). Shareholders can sell their shares at any time on the secondary market, but the market price of a share – the price quoted at any given time on the stock exchange, which reflects how well or badly the company is doing – may differ radically from its nominal, face, or par value.

At the London Stock Exchange, share transactions do not have to be settled until the account day or settlement day at the end of a two-week accounting period. This allows speculators to buy shares hoping to resell them at a higher price before they actually pay for them, or to sell shares, hoping to buy them back at a lower price.

If a company wishes to raise more money for expansion it can issue new shares. These are frequently offered to existing shareholders at less than their market price: this is known as a rights issue. Companies may also turn part of their profit into capital by issuing new shares to shareholders instead of paying dividends. This is known as a bonus issue or scrip issue or capitalisation issue in Britain, and as a stock dividend or stock split in the US. American corporations are also permitted to reduce the amount of their capital by buying back their own shares, which are then known as treasury stock; in Britain this is generally not allowed, in order to protect companies' creditors. If a company sells shares at above their par value, this amount is recorded in financial statements as share premium (GB) or paid-in surplus (US).

The Financial Times-Stock Exchange (FT-SE) 100 Share Index (known as the "Footsie") records the average value of the 100 leading British shares, and is updated every minute during trading. The most important US index is the Dow Jones Industrial Average.

1. A company can only be floated once.   TRUE/FALSE

2. Banks underwrite share issues when they want to buy the shares.   TRUE/FALSE

3. It is easier for a company to be quoted on an unlisted securities   TRUE/FALSE
   market than on a major stock exchange.

4. Unlisted companies do not publish annual reports.   TRUE/FALSE

5. The market price of a share is never the same as its nominal value.   TRUE/FALSE

6. On the London Stock Exchange it is possible to make a profit
    without ever paying anyone any money.   TRUE/FALSE

7. If a company issues new shares, it has to offer them to existing
    shareholders at a reduced price.   TRUE/FALSE

8. A scrip issue can be an alternative to paying a dividend.   TRUE/FALSE

9. American corporations with large amounts of cash can spend it
    by buying their own shares.   TRUE/FALSE

10. Companies do not have to sell their shares at their nominal value.   TRUE/FALSE

EXERCISE 2

Add appropriate words from the text to these sentences:

1. Offering shares to the public for the first time is called . . . . a company.

2. A company offering shares usually uses a merchant bank to . . . . the issue.

3. The major British companies are . . . . on the London Stock Exchange.

4. In London, share transactions have to be . . . . every two weeks.

5. The value written on a share is its . . . .

6. The value listed in the newspapers is its . . . .

Stocks and Shares 2

Complete the sentences using these words:

arbitrageurs	bears	bulls	insiders
market-makers	shareholders	stags	stockbrokers

1. People who buy stocks and shares are called . . . . in Britain, and stockholders in the USA (although most of the shares of all leading companies are held by institutional investors such as pension funds and insurance companies).

2. People who buy securities expecting their price to rise so they can resell them before the next settlement day are known as . . . .

3. People who sell shares hoping to buy them back at a lower price before the next settlement day are called . . . .

4. People who buy new share issues, hoping to resell them at a profit (if the issue is over-subscribed) are known as . . . .

5. Shareholders place their orders with, and sometimes seek advice from . . . . , who are members of the Stock Exchange, but who can work anywhere with a telephone and a computer screen connected to the Stock Exchange.

6. Brokers in turn buy shares from and sell them to . . . . , who are wholesalers in stocks and shares, and who guarantee to make a market at all times with brokers.

7. . . . . are people who occupy a position of trust within an organization and possess information not known to the public; buying or selling shares when in possession of such information that affects their price is illegal.

8. . . . . are people who buy stakes in companies involved (or expected to be involved) in takeover bids.

Types of Shares

A share (in British English) or a stock (in American English) is a security representing a portion of the nominal capital of a company. (In Britain "stock" is used to refer to either a block of shares with a nominal value of £100, or various kinds of fixed-interest securities.)

Complete the following using the phrases in the box:

barometer stocks	**blue chips**	**defensive stock**
deferred shares	**equities**	**growth stock**
mutual fund	**ordinary shares**	**participation certificates**
preference shares or **preferred stock**		

1. Another name for stocks and shares is . . . ., because all the stocks or shares of a company – or all those of a particular category – have an equal nominal value.

2. . . . . (US: common stock) are often the only kind of shares with voting rights.

3. Some companies issue . . . . which, like shares, grant their holders part of the ownership of a company, but usually without voting rights.

4. . . . ., as their name suggests, usually receive a fixed dividend, which must be paid in full before any dividend is paid on other shares. But because interest payments are tax deductible, and dividends are not, many companies now issue bonds instead.

5. . . . . (or stock), again as the name suggests, do not receive a dividend until other categories of shares have had a dividend paid on them, but might earn a higher dividend if the company does well.

6. Securities in companies that are considered to be without risk are known as . . . .

7. Widely-held stocks (e.g. blue chips or 20-year Treasury Bonds) that can be considered as indicators of present and future market performance, are known as . . . . (GB) or bellwether stocks (US).

8. A . . . . or share is one that is expected to appreciate in capital value; it usually has a high purchasing price and a low current rate of return.

9. A . . . . or income stock or share is one that offers a good yield but only a limited chance of a rise or decline in price (in an industry that is not much affected by cyclical trends).

10. A way of spreading risks is to invest in a unit trust (in Britain) or a . . . . (in the US), organizations that invest small investors' money in a wide portfolio of securities.

Market Price Idioms

Classify the following expressions according to whether you think they mean:

        (a) the price rose a little

        (b) the price rose a lot

        (c) the price fell a little

        (d) the price fell a lot

        (e) the price was almost unchanged.

1. After early losses, the Dow Jones rallied to finish ten points up.
2. Boeing shares plummeted after a door fell off a 747 taking off from Dulles International Airport and landed in the White House garden.
3. Chrysler continued to drift, finishing 75 cents down at 45 and a half.
4. CIBA-Geigy shares rocketed after the company announced the discovery of a drug that will cure people of wanting to make a fortune on the stock market.
5. Compaq stock suffered a small setback, losing $2.25.
6. EuroDisney shares sank again to FF2.35 after Mickey got caught in a mousetrap.
7. Eurotunnel shares went through the floor, finishing at 0.14.
8. Gold slipped back a little to $385.40.
9. Hill-Lewis shares took a knock, after the news that company chairman Stuart Tipping had resigned.
10. IBM stocks suffered a drop after disappointing quarterly results were released.
11. In Frankfurt, the DAX index failed to halt its slide, finishing 6 points down.
12. In Lisbon, shares were slightly weaker in light trading.
13. In Milan, shares eased slightly in subdued trading.
14. In New York, the Japanese yen slumped to 123 to the dollar.
15. In Paris, the CAC-40 recovered slightly, finishing up by 0.32%.
16. In the Philippines, shares took a tumble in heavy late trading, with the Manila Composite Index closing at 2507.33.
17. In Tokyo, shares rebounded, the Nikkei closing at 20677.83.
18. In Hong Kong, the Hang Seng Index plunged to 8269.44.
19. On Wall Street, most of the leading stocks were firmer.
20. Philip Morris also dipped, down 75 cents to $52.75.
21. Shares fell sharply across the board in Jakarta this morning.
22. Shares of Tottenham Hotspur Football Club crashed to a record low of 16p after the team lost their fourteenth successive home game on Saturday.
23. Silver was steady at six hundred and thirty-five cents an ounce.
24. The Deutschmark jumped after the weekend's election results, finishing at 0.598 against the dollar.
25. The dollar was slightly stronger in active trading yesterday.
26. The Dutch guilder leapt to an all-time high after gold was discovered in the mountains outside Amsterdam.
27. The pound revived a little, finishing 2 pfennigs up.
28. The Swiss franc advanced a little to 2.14.
29. Thirty-five points were wiped off the Footsie as shares took a beating in London.
30. Volkswagen staged a comeback, finishing up 14.

Now underline all the "up" and "down" phrases in the examples.

Rise and Fall

EXERCISE 1

Classify these verbs (from the sentences in the previous exercise), according to whether they mean *rise* or *fall*:

advance	be firm	be strong	be weak
dip	drift	drop	ease
jump	leap	plummet	plunge
rally	rebound	recover	revive
rocket	sink	slip	slump
tumble			

Four of these verbs – all in one line of the box – mean to rise after previously falling. Which are they?

Remember that *rise* and *fall* are irregular verbs: *rise - rose - risen; fall - fell - fallen.*

Remember to distinguish between *fall - fell - fallen,* and *feel - felt - felt.*

As well as the verb *rise,* English also has the verbs *raise* and *arise.*

Rise is an irregular, intransitive verb: *rise - rose - risen.* Things can rise, but you cannot rise something.

Raise is a regular, transitive verb: *raise - raised - raised.* People raise things. As well as to increase – to cause to rise – *raise* has lots of other meanings, including to collect capital, to bring up children, etc.

Arise is an irregular, intransitive verb: *arise - arose - arisen.* It means to happen or occur, or to come into existence. *Problems arose soon after the new chairman took office.*

EXERCISE 2

Complete the following sentences with the appropriate form of *rise, raise,* or *arise:*

1. A cash-flow crisis has . . . .

2. Last year we issued bonus shares and . . . . $2 million.

3. Prices have already . . . . 4% since January, and I think they're going to . . . . at the same rate until the end of the year.

4. Retail prices . . . . by 7% last year.

5. She . . . . her children all on her own while working part-time.

6. The Federal Reserve will probably . . . . interest rates by 0.5%.

7. The problem . . . . from the lack of quality control.

8. We didn't expect those difficulties to . . . . with the new product.

Bonds

EXERCISE 1

Match the responses on the right with the questions on the left:

1. So what exactly are bonds?

2. And how do they work?

3. So you have to keep them for a long time?

4. Why should that happen?

5. Oh, I see. Is that what they mean by below par?

6. But the bond's interest rate doesn't change?

7. How's that?

8. And people talk about AAA and AAB bonds, and things like that.

9. And what about gilts?

10. Not Treasury Bills?

11. And James Bond?

a. Because of changes in interest rates. For example, no-one will pay the full price for a 6% bond if new bonds are paying 10%.

b. Exactly. And the opposite, a bond whose market value is higher than its face value, is above par.

c. I knew you'd finish by saying that!

d. No, not at all. Bonds are very liquid. They can be sold on the secondary market until they mature. But of course, the price might have changed.

e. No, not unless it's a floating rate bond. The coupon, the amount of interest a bond pays, remains the same. But the yield will change.

f. No, those are short-term (three-month) instruments which the government sells to and buys from the commercial banks, to regulate the money supply.

g. That's the name they use in Britain for long-term government bonds – gilts or gilt-edged securities. In the States they call them Treasury Bonds.

h. They're securities issued by companies, governments and financial institutions when they need to borrow money.

i. Well, a bond's yield is its coupon payment expressed as a percentage of its price on the secondary market, so the yield changes if you buy or sell above or below par.

j. Well, they usually pay a fixed rate of interest and are repaid after a fixed period, known as their maturity, for example five, seven, or ten years.

k. Yes. Bond-issuing companies are given an investment grade by private ratings companies such as Standard & Poors, according to their financial situation and performance.

1	2	3	4	5	6	7	8	9	10	11

EXERCISE 2

Complete the following:

1. Companies generally use investment banks to . . . . their bonds.
2. Thereafter, they can be traded on the . . . . market.
3. The amount of interest a bond pays is often called its . . . .
4. The majority of bonds have a . . . . rate of interest.
5. A bond's . . . . depends on the price it was bought at.
6. A bond priced at 104% is described as being . . . .
7. Bonds are repaid at 100% at . . . .
8. AAA is the highest . . . .

Financial Instruments

Use the following terms to complete the sentences below:

certificates of deposit	commercial paper	currency swap
detachable warrants	forward contract	futures contract
interest-rate swap	junk bonds	off-balance-sheet transactions
participation certificates	securitization	zero coupon bonds

1. .... is short-term, discounted and unsecured corporate debt of large American banks and companies issued, usually for one to three months only, as a way of borrowing money.

2. .... pay no interest, but are sold at a large discount and ultimately redeemed at face value. They consequently yield capital gains, often taxed at a lower rate than interest, which is considered as income.

3. .... are sometimes issued with bonds, and give the buyer the right to buy the same firm's equities within a certain period. Unlike convertible bonds, the bond itself is not converted into shares.

4. .... is the process of selling packages of bank debts to third party investors as bonds. It shifts the risk of default from the bank to the new owners, and releases capital with which the bank can make new loans.

5. .... are high-yielding bonds issued by less secure companies and by companies seeking to finance leveraged buy-outs.

6. A borrower with a lot of floating loans can spread the risk via an .... with a borrower of fixed rate loans.

7. An importer who will need foreign exchange in three or six months time can buy it in advance by way of a ....

8. Banks can convert large deposits that cannot be withdrawn on demand into .... : short-term, interest-bearing securities that can be traded like a share or bond.

9. Debt swaps, letters of credit, options, etc. are all forms of financial business that need not be registered as loans on a balance sheet. They are consequently known as ....

10. Futures markets deal in contracts for standardized quantities of commodities, currencies, etc., for specific time periods. Non-standardized deals can be negotiated in an over-the-counter ....

11. Issuing .... – which grant their holder part of the ownership of a company, but without voting rights – rather than shares, diminishes the risk of takeovers.

12. Two borrowers, each with a better credit rating in their own country, but also needing foreign currency, can arrange a ....

Futures and Options

Study Exercise 1 before reading the following text:

Contracts can be made on futures markets to buy and sell currencies, various financial assets, and commodities (raw materials or primary products such as metals, cereals, tea, rubber, etc.) at a future date, but with the price fixed at the time of the deal. Currencies and commodities are also traded for immediate delivery on spot markets. Making contracts to buy or sell a commodity or financial instrument at a pre-arranged price in the future as a protection against price changes is known as hedging. Of course, this is only possible if two parties, for example, a producer and a buyer, both want to hedge, or if there are speculators who believe that they know better than the market.

Traders or speculators might wish to buy or sell a currency at a future price if it is expected to appreciate or depreciate, or if interest rates are expected to change. Prices of foodstuffs – wheat, maize, coffee, tea, sugar, cocoa, orange juice, pork bellies, etc. – are frequently affected by droughts, floods and other extreme weather conditions, which is why both producers and buyers often prefer to hedge, so as to guarantee next season's prices. When commodity prices are expected to rise, future prices are obviously higher than, or at a premium on, spot prices; when they are expected to fall they are at a discount on spot prices; when they are expected to stay the same, future prices are also higher, as they include interest costs.

As well as commodities and currencies, there is a growing futures market in stocks and shares. One can buy options giving the right to buy and sell securities at a fixed price in the future. A call option gives its holder the right but not the obligation to buy securities or a commodity or currency at a certain price during a certain period of time. A put option gives its holder the right to sell securities, currencies, commodities, etc. at a certain price during a certain period of time.

The buyer of a share option pays a premium per share to the seller, and only risks this amount. The seller of an option (known as the writer) risks losing an unlimited amount of money, depending on the performance of the underlying share, especially if he or she does not actually possess it. If you expect the value of a share that you own to fall below its current price, you can buy a put option at this price (or higher): if the price falls, you can still sell your shares at this price. Alternatively, you could write a call option giving someone else the right to buy the share at the current price: if the market price remains below this price, no-one will take up the option, and you earn the premium.

On the contrary, if you think a share will rise, you can buy a call option giving the right to buy at the current price, hoping to buy and resell the share at a profit, or to sell this option. Or you can write a put option giving someone else the right to sell the shares at the current price: if the market price remains above this, no-one will exercise the option, so you earn the premium.

The price at which the holder of a call/put option may buy/sell the underlying security is known as its exercise or strike price. A call (put) option has intrinsic value if its exercise price is below (above) the current market price of the underlying share. Call options with an exercise price below the underlying share's current market price, and put options with an exercise price above the share's market price, are described as being "in-the-money". On the contrary, call options with an exercise price higher than a share's current market price, and put options with an exercise price lower than the share's market price, are "out-of-the-money".

EXERCISE 1

Decide whether the following statements are TRUE or FALSE:

1. The price of a futures contract is determined at the moment the   TRUE/FALSE
    contract is made.

2. Hedging is another name for speculating.   TRUE/FALSE

3. Futures prices are always higher than spot prices, because they   TRUE/FALSE
    contain interest charges.

4. In options, 'call' means 'buy' and 'put' means 'sell'.   TRUE/FALSE

5. The amount of money one can make or lose on an options contract   TRUE/FALSE
    is determined at the moment the contract is made.

6. You can sell an option to sell an asset you do not actually possess.   TRUE/FALSE

7. If you think a share will rise, you can profit by buying a call option   TRUE/FALSE
    or writing a put option giving someone else the right to sell the shares
    at the current price.

8. If you think the value of a share you own will fall below its current   TRUE/FALSE
    price, you can profitably buy a call option at this price (or higher)
    or write a put option.

9. A put option has intrinsic value if its exercise price is above the   TRUE/FALSE
    current market price of the underlying share.

10. A call option with an exercise price below the underlying share's   TRUE/FALSE
    current market price is "out-of-the-money".

EXERCISE 2

Match up the following words (using them more than once if necessary) to make up at least ten two-word nouns:

call	contract	financial	forward	futures
instrument	market	materials	option	price
primary	product	raw	spot	strike

EXERCISE 3

Match up the following words or expressions to make eight pairs of opposites:

call option	discount	drought	exercise price
flood	futures market	hedging	in-the-money
market price	obligation	out-of-the-money	premium
put option	right	speculation	spot market

Review – Bonds and Shares

Ten of the following twenty-one words and expressions have a direct relation to bonds, and ten others are more likely to be used in relation to stocks or shares. One word logically applies to both categories. Make two lists:

above par	**accounting period**	**blue chip**
broker	**bull**	**convertible**
coupon	**crash**	**debt**
dividend	**Dow-Jones**	**equity**
floating rate	**flotation**	**insider**
interest	**investment grade**	**junk**
maturity	**redeem**	**zero coupon**

Bonds   Shares

. . . .

. . . .

. . . .

. . . .

. . . .

. . . .

. . . .

. . . .

. . . .

. . . .

Both bonds and shares

. . . .

Review – Securities

In this wordbox you should be able to find 23 words, either horizontal (left to right), vertical (top to bottom) or diagonal (top left to bottom right), including:

1. 3 types of investors, named after animals

2. 6 names of securities

3. 10 verbs related to securities

4. 4 words relating to the income investors receive from securities.

B	U	L	L	I	S	S	U	E	Y	C
E	U	J	Q	N	H	T	E	Z	I	A
A	P	Y	B	T	A	O	A	L	E	L
R	U	D	O	E	R	C	F	G	L	L
E	T	E	N	R	E	K	U	N	D	I
T	R	A	D	E	O	P	T	I	O	N
U	I	L	E	S	A	I	U	E	E	V
R	G	I	L	T	N	C	R	K	N	E
N	M	D	I	V	I	D	E	N	D	S
H	E	D	G	E	W	R	I	T	E	T

Review – Financial Instruments

Add the words and expressions that complete the following sentences to the wordbox:

1. A (10,5) receives a dividend before the other classes of share.
2. An (8,8) is one issued by a fairly new or small company, sold on a smaller stock exchange with fewer regulations than the big stock exchanges.
3. A (5,5) is one of three names for new shares distributed to shareholders instead of a dividend.
4. A (7) is sometimes issued with a bond, giving the holder the right to buy the same company's shares at a certain price.
5. A (4,4) is one that is considered risky, but which pays a high rate of interest.
6. A (4,6,4) pays no interest, but instead is issued at a discount (and of course redeemed at 100%).
7. An (6) gives the right to buy or sell an asset at a certain price on a certain date.
8. A (4) is the exchange of one security, currency, etc. for another.
9. A (4) is a bond issued by the British government.
10. A (8,4) is a short-term security issued by the Bank of England to regulate the money supply.
11. An (8,5) is the most common type of equity.
12. A (6,5) is one whose owner is not registered with the issuing company.
13. A (6,5) is one whose market price is expected to rise in the future.
14. A (8) is a loan to buy property, with the property (house, apartment, etc.) serving as a guarantee for the loan.
15. A (4,4) is a security in a large, safe, profitable company.
16. (6,5) is the American equivalent of ordinary shares in Britain.
17. A (8,5) does not receive any dividend payment until after other categories of shares have received theirs.
18. A (9) is a bond issued by a company and secured by the company's assets.
19. A (6) is a contract to deliver a commodity, security, currency, etc. at a pre-arranged date, with the price fixed when the contract is made.
20. A (6,5) consists of new shares offered at below their nominal value to existing shareholders.

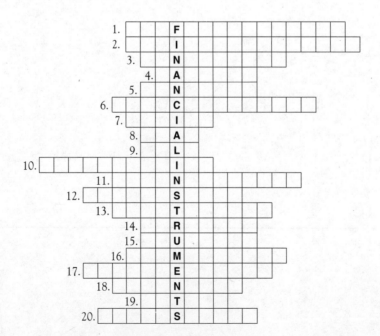

Financial Ratios

A ratio is the number obtained when one number is divided by another. Various financial ratios are used to measure profitability, solvency, liquidity, efficiency, etc.

Match the explanations on this page with the ratios on page 80.

The **current ratio** (or working capital) measures liquidity - i.e. having enough cash to meet short-term obligations. It shows if a business can pay its most urgent debts.

The **quick ratio** (or **acid test ratio**) provides a more accurate picture of short-term solvency by considering completely liquid assets.

A company's **profit margin** or **return on sales** is the percentage difference between sales income and the cost of sales.

Productivity shows the amount of work or sales per employee.

Earnings per share relates the company's profits to the number of ordinary shares it has issued.

The **price/earnings ratio (PER)** reflects the market's opinion of a company's revenues, earnings and dividends: the higher it is, the more investors are optimistic about the company's future prospects.

A company's **debt/equity ratio**, or **gearing** compares the amount of debt to the firm's own capital. A highly-geared company is one that has a lot of debt compared to equity.

Interest cover or **times interest earned** shows whether funds are available to pay long-term debt costs.

Dividend cover or the **dividend payout ratio** shows the percentage of income paid out to shareholders (or the number of times the net profits available for distribution exceed the dividend actually paid).

Return on equity shows profit compared to shareholders' capital.

Return on total assets shows profit compared to all of a company's capital, whether debt or equity.

A company's **market/book ratio** is current stock market value divided by the amount invested by shareholders. (This equals the return on equity multiplied by the price/earnings ratio.)

Note
The American term for *gearing* is *leverage*.

What are the names of these ratios? Try not to look back at page 79.

1. . . . .
$$\frac{\text{common stock dividend}}{\text{net income}}$$

2. . . . .
$$\frac{\text{current assets}}{\text{current liabilities}}$$

3. . . . .
$$\frac{\text{distributable profit}}{\text{number of shares}}$$

4. . . . .
$$\frac{\text{liquid assets}}{\text{current liabilities}}$$

5. . . . .
$$\frac{\text{(long-term) loan capital}}{\text{shareholders' equity or net assets}}$$

6. . . . .
$$\frac{\text{market value of stock, per share}}{\text{past year's earnings per share}}$$

7. . . . .
$$\frac{\text{market value x number of shares}}{\text{nominal value x number of shares}}$$

8. . . . .
$$\frac{\text{pre-tax profit}}{\text{interest charges}}$$

9. . . . .
$$\frac{\text{pre-tax profit}}{\text{owners' equity}}$$

10. . . . .
$$\frac{\text{pre-tax profit}}{\text{sales}}$$

11. . . . .
$$\frac{\text{pre-tax profit}}{\text{total assets}}$$

12. . . . .
$$\frac{\text{sales volume}}{\text{number (or wages) of employees}}$$

Takeovers

Complete the texts with the words in the boxes:

Sooner or later, all companies need to introduce new products and services. Large companies often have the choice of innovating – developing new products, services or markets themselves – or of buying another, smaller company with successful products. If the other company is too big to acquire, another possibility is to merge or amalgamate with it. Other reasons for taking over or combining with other companies include:

diversifying	**optimizing**	**rationalizing**
reducing	**reinforcing**	**searching**

1. . . . . your company's position;
2. . . . . competition;
3. . . . . production;
4. . . . . the use of a plant or invested capital;
5. . . . . products or markets; and
6. . . . . for synergy (the belief that together the companies will produce more than the sum of the two separate parts).

buy	**grow**	**increase**	**launch**	**persuade**	**sell**

A company that wants to (7) . . . . or diversify can (8) . . . . a raid – in other words, simply (9) . . . . a large quantity of another company's shares on the stock exchange. A "dawn raid" consists of buying shares through several brokers early in the morning, before the market has time to notice the rising price, and before speculators join in. This will immediately (10) . . . . the share price, and may (11) . . . . a sufficient number of other shareholders to (12) . . . . for the raider to take control of the company.

board	**friendly**	**hostile**	**poison pill**	**white knight**

If a raid is not, or would not be, successful, a predator can make a takeover bid: a public offer to a company's shareholders to buy their shares, at a particular price during a particular period. A (13) . . . . takeover has the consent of the directors of the company whose shares are being acquired; a (14) . . . . takeover bid is one undertaken against the wishes of the (15) . . . . of directors. Defences against a hostile takeover include the (16) . . . . – a defensive action taken to repel a raider, such as changing the share voting structure or the board of directors, or spending all the company's cash reserves. If measures such as these do not work, a company can at least attempt to find a (17) . . . . – another buyer whom they prefer.

Phrasal Verbs – Takeovers

EXERCISE 1

Match up the phrasal verbs on the left with the verbs that have a similar meaning on the right:

1. act on advice	a. accept an offer
2. adhere to principles	b. accumulate capital
3. branch out	c. acquire a company
4. build up capital	d. await with pleasure
5. cash in on	e. collapse
6. draw up a plan	f. defeat
7. fall through	g. diversify
8. fight off	h. follow advice
9. get away with something	i. invent
10. look after	j. prepare a plan
11. look forward to	k. profit from
12. make up	l. protect
13. rely on *or* count on someone	m. respect principles
14. take over a company	n. succeed in doing something wrong
15. take up an offer	o. trust someone

1	2	3	4	5	6	7	8	9	10	11	12	13	14	15

EXERCISE 2

Use the phrasal verbs in the left-hand column to complete the text below (using each verb once only). You may need to use the past tense, the past participle or the present continuous form.

When we tried to (1) . . . . MacKenzie PLC we were all (2) . . . . an easy victory. We thought that most of their shareholders would (3) . . . . the chance of a quick profit. But the directors were determined to (4) . . . . our bid. They (5) . . . . a lot of untrue stories about our company, and criticized our last Annual Report, claiming that we hadn't (6) . . . . Generally Accepted Accounting Principles, and that our accountants had (7) . . . . a lot of window dressing. They were able to convince their shareholders that they could (8) . . . . them (the current management) to (9) . . . . their interests better than we could. Over the years, they had obviously (10) . . . . a lot of respect from their shareholders, who (11) . . . . the board of directors' advice, and didn't (12). . . . . our offer. Thus the whole deal (13) . . . . But we are now (14) . . . . alternative plans to (15) . . . . in a new direction.

Word Partnerships – Capital

EXERCISE 1

All the words below can be combined with *capital* in a two-word noun or adjective, e.g. *capital-intensive, venture capital*. Add the word *capital* either before or after each of the words below:

1. . . . . asset . . . .
2. . . . . expenditure . . . .
3. . . . . formation . . . .
4. . . . . gains . . . .
5. . . . . goods . . . .
6. . . . . human . . . .
7. . . . . intensive . . . .
8. . . . . investment . . . .
9. . . . . issued . . . .
10. . . . . market . . . .

11. . . . . nominal . . . .
12. . . . . ratio . . . .
13. . . . . share . . . .
14. . . . . sum . . . .
15. . . . . transfer . . . .
16. . . . . turnover . . . .
17. . . . . uncalled . . . .
18. . . . . unissued . . . .
19. . . . . venture . . . .
20. . . . . working . . . .

EXERCISE 2

Now complete the following ten sentences:

1. . . . . are those that are used in the making of other goods.

2. . . . . describes activities which require a great deal of capital investment.

3. . . . . has been issued but not yet paid for (when shareholders are given the possibility of paying in instalments).

4. . . . . include inheritances, and so on, and are usually taxed at a special rate.

5. . . . . include profits from investments, the sale of assets, and so on, and are often subject to a special tax.

6. . . . . is a term that acknowledges the value of education, training, and so on.

7. . . . . is capital that is allowed according to a company's Memorandum of Association, but which has not yet been offered for sale.

8. . . . . is invested in new enterprises.

9. . . . . is the money required to finance a company's everyday operations.

10. A . . . . is one that cannot be sold or turned into cash as it is required for making or selling the firm's products.

Leveraged Buyouts

EXERCISE 1

Match the responses on the right with the sentences on the left:

1. What's the difference between a takeover bid and an LBO?

2. Borrowed from where?

3. Ah-huh. Guess what my next question is?

4. OK, so you borrow money and buy a company. Then what?

5. Uh?

6. And then you pay back the bank or the bond-holders?

7. Sounds easy.

8. Oh I see. So it can go wrong. Just one more thing . . .

9. Forget it!

a. Exactly. And make a profit in the process.

b. LBO is short for "leveraged buyout." It involves buying a company with a lot of borrowed money.

c. Not an appalling joke about "elbows", I hope?

d. OK. They're bonds that are considered to be fairly risky but which pay a high rate of interest. People buy them because the high returns generally compensate the risk of default.

e. Well, it can go wrong. If there's a recession or a stock market crash it makes it more difficult to sell the assets, and if you have less sales revenue, it becomes harder to pay the interest on the borrowed money.

f. Well, you choose a large, badly-managed, inefficient corporation or conglomerate, or a company with huge cash reserves, or whose assets are worth more than its stock market value. You buy it, restructure it, and sell the profitable bits. It's called asset-stripping.

g. Wherever you can get it. You can try to get an ordinary loan from a bank, or you can try to sell junk bonds.

h. You sell it again.

1		2		3		4		5		6		7		8	

EXERCISE 2

Add appropriate words to these sentences:

1. Leverage means using a high proportion of . . . . money.

2. LBOs are often . . . . by junk bonds.

3. The people who try LBOs compare the value of a company's assets with its . . . .

4. The profit in an LBO often comes from . . . .

5. LBOs have led to several . . . . being split up.

Insider Dealing Puzzle

Company A was planning to take over its big rival Company B, and had borrowed £20 million from a British merchant bank. The day before it announced its bid, the price of Company B's shares unexpectedly rose 10%. Stock exchange investigators suspected insider dealing: somebody in the bank was profiting from the information that a takeover was going to increase Company B's share price, and had bought a lot of them. At the end of the inquiry, the chief investigator gave journalists the following information, and told them to work out for themselves who was guilty.

1. There were five suspects, of five different *nationalities*, working in five different *departments* in a row of five neighbouring *offices* along the same corridor in the bank. Each banker drives a *different car*, and has a *different expensive hobby*.
2. The American collects post-impressionist paintings.
3. The banker in the middle office drives power boats.
4. The banker with the BMW is in the next office to the one who works in mergers and acquisitions (who is not necessarily guilty).
5. The banker with the Ferrari works in the office immediately between those of the Jaguar driver, and the Maserati driver, who has the right-hand office.
6. The banker with the Maserati collects expensive Bordeaux wines.
7. The banker with the Mercedes works in the office next to the one who specializes in underwriting share issues.
8. The British banker, in the left-hand office, works next door to the person with a Mercedes.
9. The Ferrari driver regularly goes on safari hunting trips.
10. The Frenchman is a bond dealer.
11. The Jaguar driver, who is German, advises customers about shares.
12. The Swiss banker has a Maserati.
13. Now, said the chief investigator, two of these people are guilty. One of them flies a helicopter in his spare time, and the other specializes in financing international trade. Who are they?

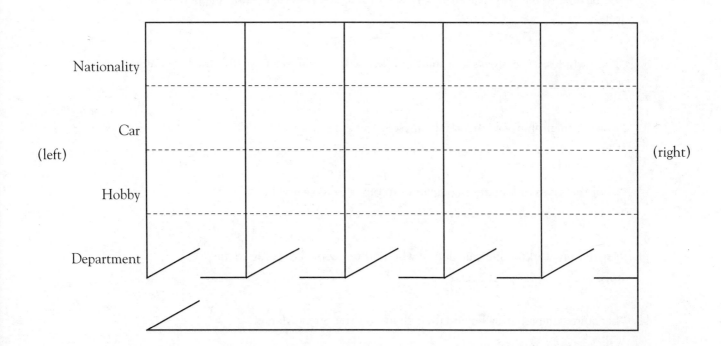

(left)   (right)

Nationality

Car

Hobby

Department

Business People

Match the statements with the job titles in the box:

accountant	actuary	arbitrageur	auditor
broker	cambist	economist	entrepreneur
liquidator	market-maker	raider	sole trader

1. "I've set up my own business and now employ a lot of people."
    JOB: . . . .

2. "I buy and sell securities for my customers."
    JOB: . . . .

3. "I buy the shares of companies that I think will be involved in takeover bids."
    JOB: . . . .

4. "I check and evaluate financial records prepared by other people."
    JOB: . . . .

5. "I deal in foreign currencies."
    JOB: . . . .

6. "I keep financial records and prepare financial statements."
    JOB: . . . .

7. "I'll be able to tell you tomorrow why what I forecast yesterday didn't happen today!"
    JOB: . . . .

8. "I'm a wholesaler in stocks and shares. I deal with stockbrokers at the stock exchange."
    JOB: . . . .

9. "I own a small shop which I run by myself."
    JOB: . . . .

10. "I sell the assets of bankrupt companies in order to repay creditors."
    JOB: . . . .

11. "I spend my working life calculating when other people are going to die!"
    JOB: . . . .

12. "I acquire companies by buying their shares on the Stock Market."
    JOB: . . . .

Economic Issues

"The purpose of studying economics is not to acquire a
set of ready-made answers to economic questions,
but to learn how to avoid being deceived by economists."
JOAN ROBINSON

Basic Economic Terms 1

Use the following terms to complete the definitions below:

aggregate demand	**econometrics**	**endogenous**
equilibrium	**exogenous**	**externalities**
factors of production	**gross national product (GNP)**	
macroeconomics	**microeconomics**	

1. . . . . (or inputs) are resources used by firms in their production processes, namely land and the natural resources in it, labour, capital, and (in recent definitions) information.

2. (or spillovers) are costs imposed on others without their receiving compensation, or benefits received by others without their paying the proper costs.

3. . . . . concerns the economic factors affecting individual consumers and companies.

4. is a state of balance, for example, when supply meets demand.

5. . . . . is the application of mathematical and statistical models to economic theories and problems.

6. . . . . is the study and analysis of the economy as a whole.

7. . . . . is the total amount spent in a country by consumers, companies, and the government.

8. . . . . is the total wealth earned or created in a country in a year.

9. . . . . means coming from or controlled from within, e.g. variables that are totally under the control of a company, a government, etc.

10. means coming from or controlled from without; uncontrollable variables.

Basic Economic Terms 2

Which twelve terms in the box are defined in the sentences below?

aggregate supply	**balance of payments**	**capital**
cost of living	**economic**	**economical**
economize	**economy**	**fiscal**
free enterprise	**fluctuate**	**inflation**
inputs	**market**	**monetarism**
protectionism	**scarcity**	**standard of living**

1. . . . .

   Adjective meaning of or relating to an economy or economics.

2. . . . .

   Adjective meaning related to public (i.e. government) finances (taxation, expenditure, etc.).

3. . . . .

   Adjective meaning using a minimum of resources; or cheap.

4. . . . .

   A rise in the general level of prices, and an increase in the money supply.

5. . . . .

   A shortage of something; insufficient supply to meet demand.

6. . . . .

   The accumulated stock of goods used for the production of further goods (and the money required to purchase them).

7. . . . .

   A measure of the amount of money that has to be paid for essentials such as food, accommodation, heating, clothing, etc.

8. . . . .

   A measure of the amount of disposable income that people have to spend on both necessities and luxuries.

9. . . . .

   The difference between what a country pays for its imports and receives for its exports.

10. . . . .

   The practice of restricting imports in order to increase the sales of domestic products.

11. . . . .

   To change constantly, to show irregular variation.

12. . . . .

   To save money, to reduce expenses, to reduce an amount normally used.

Describing Graphs

Here are the words and phrases you need to talk about trends using graphs. Make sure you can translate these into your own language.

UP – verbs

go up	take off	shoot up	soar	jump
increase	rise	grow	improve	rocket

UP – nouns

an increase	a rise	a growth	an improvement
an upturn	a surge	an upsurge	an upward trend

DOWN – verbs

go/come down	fall	fall off	drop	slump
decline	decrease	slip	plummet	shrink

DOWN – nouns

a fall	a decrease	a decline	a drop
a downturn	a downward trend		

NO CHANGE – verbs

remain stable	level off	stay at the same level
remain constant	stagnate	stabilise

AT THE TOP – verbs

reach a peak	peak	top out

AT THE BOTTOM – verbs

reach a low point	bottom out	recover

DEGREES OF CHANGE

Adjectives: dramatic, considerable, sharp, significant, substantial, moderate, slight

Adverbs: dramatically, considerably, sharply, significantly, substantially, moderately, slightly

SPEED OF CHANGE

abrupt	sudden	rapid	quick	steady	gradual	slow

PREPOSITIONS

a rise *from* £1m *to* £2m	to increase *by* 50%
to fall *by* 30%	an increase *of* 7.5 per cent *over* last year

Study the following graphs. Complete the descriptions with information from them and language from the previous page. Several answers are possible. Check your answers with those in the answer key or discuss them with your teacher.

GRAPH·1 Profits 1967–1982

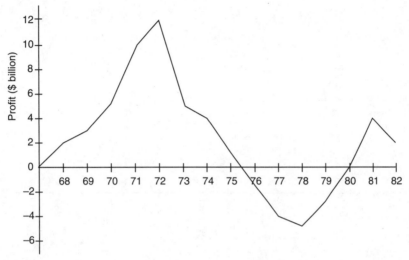

The company came out of the red in 1968 after which there was a (1) . . . . in profits every year for four years. Profits reached (2) . . . . in 1972, but in 1973, the year of the oil crisis, there was a (3) . . . . The (4) . . . . trend in 1974 was smaller, but after that profits continued to (5) . . . . for four years. The company made a $5 billion loss in 1978, after which the figures (6) . . . . for three years, before (7) . . . . again in 1982.

GRAPH 2 Sales Years 1–12

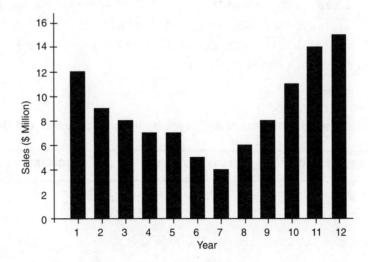

The year after we took over the company sales were good, at $12m, but the second year they (1) . . . . In fact, they dropped (2) . . . . 25%. Sales (3) . . . . for another two years, (4) . . . . for one year, and then (5) . . . . again twice. Since then,   there has been a (6) . . . . growth for five years. In fact in just four years, sales rose (7) . . . . $4m (8) . . . . $14m, an increase (9) . . . . 250%.

The Business Cycle

Look at the graph below which illustrates fluctuations in domestic investment in the USA as a percentage of potential Gross National Product, from 1929-1988. The level of investment is clearly linked to the business cycle. Insert the words in the boxes in the texts below.

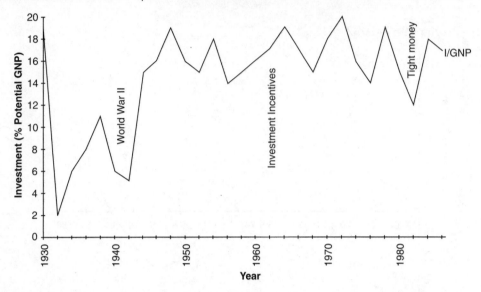

EXERCISE 1

boom	contracted	depression
downturns	expanded	peak
recession	recovery	upturns

A period of stock market speculation ended dramatically in October 1929 with the infamous Wall Street Crash. There followed a dramatic (1) . . . . The economy (2) . . . . again after World War II. There was a series of (3) . . . . and (4) . . . . in the 1950s. There was a long (5) . . . . in the 1960s. Investment reached a (6) . . . . in 1972, just before the first oil crisis. There was a (7) . . . . in 1975 and the economy (8) . . . . again in 1982, but each time there was a rapid (9) . . . .

EXERCISE 2

Now complete the following sentences, using expressions from page 90, and these conjunctions:

as a consequence of	as a result of	because	owing to

1. Investment . . . . in 1930 . . . . the Crash of 1929.

2. Private investment . . . . during World War II . . . . money was needed for the war effort.

3. There was a . . . . in investment in the 1960s . . . . the government's incentive policies.

4. Investment . . . . at the end of the 1970s . . . . the Federal Reserve's tight monetary policy.

The Three Sectors of the Economy

EXERCISE 1

Match the following questions and answers:

1. What do we mean by the primary sector of the economy?

2. What happens to the food extracted in the primary sector?

3. So what's the secondary sector?

4. So people in the secondary sector make things?

5. And the tertiary sector?

6. Why is the number of people working in the primary sector regularly declining?

7. And why is the secondary sector getting smaller in many of these countries?

8. But not tertiary services?

a. Because agricultural methods are always becoming more efficient. Western Europe and the USA already produce too much food with only 3% of the population working on the land.

b. Because much manufacturing can be carried out more cheaply in low-wage economies, for example in East and South-East Asian countries like China, Hong Kong, Taiwan, South Korea, Malaya and Vietnam.

c. Agriculture and the extraction of raw materials from the earth (coal-mining, drilling for oil) or the sea (fishing).

d. It includes the commercial services that enable industry to produce and distribute goods to their final consumers (trade, banking, insurance, warehousing, transport, communications, advertising, and so on), as well as activities like education, health care and tourism.

e. It involves the transformation of raw materials into finished products.

f. Not if the activities require a lot of training, education, know-how and technology.

g. Only some of them. Manufacturing companies also employ finance and marketing managers, administrative staff, maintenance staff, and so on.

h. Some of it, such as fresh fruit or fish, is consumed almost immediately after extraction; the rest serves as raw material for the secondary sector.

1		2		3		4		5		6		7		8	

EXERCISE 2

Add verbs in the correct form to the following sentences.

1. Raw materials are . . . . from the ground and then either . . . . , or . . . . into finished goods.

2. Before finished goods are sold they often have to be . . . . , ... , etc.

Phrasal Verbs – Recession

EXERCISE 1

Match up the phrasal verbs on the left with the verbs that have a similar meaning on the right:

1.	bottom out	a.	accept (job, responsibility, etc.)
2.	bring out	b.	continue
3.	carry on	c.	decline
4.	carry out	d.	dismiss
5.	close down	e.	establish
6.	count on	f.	have confidence in
7.	cut back on	g.	increase (prices)
8.	fall off	h.	introduce something new
9.	lay off	i.	postpone, delay
10.	level off	j.	reach the lowest point
11.	look through	k.	read quickly
12.	look for	l.	reduce
13.	mark up	m.	reduce in size
14.	pull out of	n.	shut
15.	put off	o.	stabilize
16.	scale down	p.	try to find
17.	set up	q.	do or undertake
18.	take on	r.	withdraw from

1		2		3		4		5		6		7		8		9	
10		11		12		13		14		15		16		17		18	

EXERCISE 2

Use each of the phrasal verbs above once to complete the text. You may need to use the past tense, the past participle or the present continuous form.

After three years of rapid growth, sales began to (1) . . . . Then, with the recession, they (2) . . . . dramatically. We had to (3) . . . . the factory in Ireland, and (4) . . . . sixty people. That left a lot of machine workers (5) . . . . a job in one small town. They (6) . . . . the newspapers every day, but there weren't many job vacancies. The unemployed had to (7) . . . . any kind of casual work they could find.

We also had to (8) . . . . staff in the London office, and reconsider the whole British operation that we'd (9) . . . . only five years before. Some of the American managers wanted to (10) . . . . the British market entirely, and to (11) . . . . our whole European business. Instead we have (12) . . . . a restructuring, and (13) . . . . all our plans for expansion, and for (14) . . . . new products. We're trying to (15) . . . . as best we can. We might even have to (16) . . . . our prices a little, hoping we can (17) . . . . our customers' brand loyalty. At least there are some signs that the recession has (18) . . . .

Political Economy

Which ten terms in the box are defined in the sentences below?

austerity	**capitalism**	**crowd out**	**demand management**
deregulation	**infrastructure**	**interference**	**intervention**
laissez-faire	**market economy**	**market failures**	**mixed economy**
monetarism	**planned economy**	**private sector**	**public sector**
recession	**regulation**	**stagnant**	**supply-side theory**

1. . . . .

   an economy with both private and public sectors.

2. . . . .

   a word used to describe economic policies and measures designed to reduce inflation, the quantity of imports, government spending, and so on.

3. . . . .

   all nationalized industries or services, such as education, health care, justice, public transport.

4. . . . .

   situations in which free competition and the effects of supply and demand do not operate (e.g. monopolies and oligopolies, and externalities).

5. . . . .

   the belief that the economy works best when the state does not plan, control, or interfere.

6. . . . .

   the ending or relaxing of legal regulations or restrictions in a particular industry (e.g. finance, television).

7. . . . .

   the Keynesian policy of stimulating an economy in a period of recession, and contracting the economy if it overheats.

8. . . . .

   the neutral term that describes governmental action in the economy.

9. . . . .

   all the services such as roads, railways, electricity, telephones, etc. that exist in developed countries.

10. . . . .

   reduce the amount of money available for private investment by increasing government borrowing.

Competition

Choose the correct alternatives to complete the text:

The rare situation in which all producers are too small to affect the market price is called (1) . . . . Where even one producer can affect the price of a good by increasing or withholding output there is (2) . . . . A market with only one producer who can fix an artificial price is called a (3) . . . . The opposite situation, where there is only one buyer – e.g. for defence systems – is described as (4) . . . .

The situation where there are only a few sellers is called (5) . . . . This frequently arises in manufacturing industry because of economies of scale – continuously declining unit costs as production increases – and the cost barriers of entering an industry. A (6) . . . . is where companies in the same industry collaborate by coordinating prices, sharing out markets, etc. In many countries, including the USA, this is illegal, under (7) . . . . The situation in which there are only a small number of relatively large buyers in a market is (8) . . . .

Some monopolies are legal. For example, inventors are granted (9) . . . . that give them monopolistic privileges for a certain length of time. There are also natural monopolies, such as water, gas, electricity and telephones where it may not be economic to have a large number of competing companies laying cables or pipes to the same consumers. Consequently, (10) . . . . companies such as these are frequently granted monopolies, but with prices regulated by the government.

1. a. communism	b. oligopoly	c. perfect competition
2. a. capitalism	b. monopoly	c. imperfect competition
3. a. competitive advantage	b. monopoly	c. monopsony
4. a. nationalization	b. monopoly	c. monopsony
5. a. an oligopoly	b. an oligopsony	c. a recession
6. a. cartel	b. conglomerate	c. conspiracy
7. a. anti-trust laws	b. honesty laws	c. trust laws
8. a. a concentration	b. an oligopoly	c. an oligopsony
9. a. licences	b. patents	c. trademarks
10. a. useful	b. utility	c. utilitarian

"Done it! All the little dots are in the centre circle."

Government Spending

Sentences 1 to 10 make up a short text about government spending. Complete each sentence, by taking a middle part from the second box and an end from the third box:

1. If tax revenues are higher
2. If, on the contrary, government expenditures exceed
3. A structural surplus or deficit
4. A cyclical surplus or deficit, on the other hand,
5. Budget deficits have to be funded by the sale of government bonds,
6. The higher the amount of government bonds sold in a country,
7. Neo-classical economists
8. On the other hand, if the money supply is expanded,
9. This is partly due to the acceleration principle,
10. But of course everybody knows

---

a. called gilt-edged securities in Britain,
b. call this "crowding out",
c. increased government spending
d. is the result of government policies such as
e. is the result of the business cycle:
f. money collected by taxes,
g. than government spending,
h. that increasing the money supply
i. the less capital is available
j. which is that increased demand for consumer goods

---

k. a country has a budget deficit.
l. a country has a budget surplus.
m. almost inevitably leads to inflation.
n. and Treasury bonds in the USA.
o. and use it as an argument against Keynesian fiscal policies.
p. can raise output and investment, at least in the short term.
q. changes in spending or revenues caused by a boom or a slump.
r. for private sector investment.
s. produces a greater increased demand for capital goods.
t. tax rates, welfare and defence spending, and so on.

Beginning	1	2	3	4	5	6	7	8	9	10
Middle										
Ending										

Inflation

Complete the text by using the following words:

assets	**consumer**	**debts**	**deflation**
excess	**employment**	**hyperinflation**	**interest**
producers	**restrictions**	**spending**	**supply**
	unemployment	**weighted**	

Inflation is a rise in the general level of prices. It is caused by an (1) . . . . of demand over supply, and is related to an increase in the money (2) . . . . Single-digit inflation is usually described by economists as moderate inflation. Double or triple-digit inflation, which some countries have survived for quite long periods, is known as galloping inflation. Inflation of four or more digits, as in Germany in the early 1920s, and Argentina in the early 1980s, is known as (3) . . . .

Prices in general tend to remain at the same anticipated level unless there are demand-pull or cost-push shocks. If aggregate demand exceeds what a country can produce at full (4) . . . . , prices will rise (including wages, the price of labour): this is demand-pull inflation. But, for the last fifty years, costs have pushed up prices and wages, even in recessions and periods of high (5) . . . . : this is cost-push inflation. Cost-push inflation is caused, for example, when unions demand wages that employers cannot afford or when oil (6) . . . . are able to raise their prices.

The opposite of inflation, when prices fall (generally for short periods), is (7) . . . . Government policies can be inflationary (often by accident), disinflationary or reflationary. Disinflationary policies might be aimed at slowing down price inflation or at reducing imports; they involve reducing demand by raising taxation and/or cutting government (8) . . . . Reflationary policies, on the contrary, involve revitalizing a sluggish economy by increasing consumer demand, either by cutting taxes or raising benefits, or relaxing monetary and credit (9) . . . .

Inflation is measured by the retail price index (RPI) in Britain and the (10) . . . . price index (CPI) in the US. These measure the cost of a 'basket' of goods and services, including food, clothing, housing, fuel, transport and medical care. The individual items in price indices are (11) . . . . , meaning that allowance is made for their relative importance in people's spending.

Unless inflation is both balanced (affecting all prices and costs equally) and anticipated, it distorts relative prices, tax rates and real (12) . . . . rates. Unexpected inflation tends to benefit people with fixed nominal interest rate (13) . . . . , and to disadvantage creditors and people with fixed nominal interest rate (14) . . . . or non-index-linked pensions.

1. What is the inflation rate in your country at present?
2. Can you give current examples of double and triple-digit inflation?
3. What is your government's policy at the moment? Does it seem to be more concerned with price stability or with reducing unemployment?

Unemployment

Match the following terms with the definitions below, and then use them to label the drawings:

classical unemployment	**seasonal unemployment**
cyclical unemployment	**structural unemployment**
frictional unemployment	**voluntary unemployment**

1. . . . . exists in trades or occupations where work fluctuates according to the time of year.
2. . . . . exists when people choose not to work, often because they cannot find jobs that pay enough money (e.g. more than social security benefits).
3. . . . . is temporary unemployment that arises when people voluntarily leave a job to look for another one.
4. . . . . is the loss of jobs caused when wages are too high.
5. . . . . occurs during recessions, when the overall demand for labour declines.
6. . . . . occurs when the skills of available workers do not match the jobs vacant.

I lost my job with 4,000 other people when they closed down the coal mine. 	It's crazy – the only jobs available round here pay less than I get from Social Security. 
1.	**4.**

I work with a travelling circus in the summer, but it's just closed for the winter. 	I'm a skilled electrician, but there's such a slump in the construction industry right now that I'm out of work. 
2.	**5.**

The union went on strike for an 8% pay rise. They got it, but the company laid off ten of us. 	I left my job last week after an argument with my boss. I'm sure I can find something better. 
3.	**6.**

Taxation

Choose the correct words to complete each sentence:

1. The tax on wages and salaries (and business profits in the US) is called . . . . In Britain the tax on business profits is called corporation tax.

   a. direct tax   b. income tax   c. wealth tax

2. A tax that is levied at a higher rate on higher incomes is called a . . . . tax.

   a. progressive   b. regressive   c. value-added

3. Property taxes, sales taxes, customs duties on imports, and excise duties on tobacco, alcoholic drinks, petrol, etc. are . . . . taxes.

   a. direct   b. indirect   c. value-added

4. Most sales taxes are slightly . . . . because poorer people need to spend a larger proportion of their income on consumption than the rich.

   a. progressive   b. regressive   c. repressive

5. A sales tax collected at each stage of production, excluding the already-taxed costs from previous stages, is called a . . . .

   a. sales tax   b. value-added tax   c. added-value tax

6. Profits made from the sale of assets are liable to a . . . . tax.

   a. capital gains   b. capital transfer   c. wealth

7. Gifts and inheritances are usually liable to . . . . tax.

   a. capital gains   b. capital transfer   c. wealth

8. Reducing the amount of tax you pay to a legal minimum is called . . . .

   a. fiscal policy   b. tax avoidance   c. tax evasion

9. Making false declarations is called . . . . and is obviously illegal.

   a. creative accounting   b. tax avoidance   c. tax evasion

10. Bringing forward capital expenditure (on new factories, machines, and so on) so that at the end of the year all the profits have been used up is known as making a . . . .

    a. mistake   b. tax haven   c. tax loss

11. Multinational companies often set up their head offices in low-tax countries such as Liechtenstein, Monaco, the Cayman Islands, and the Bahamas, known as . . . .

    a. tax havens   b. tax heavens   c. tax shelters

12. Criminal multinationals such as the Mafia tend to pass money through a series of companies in very complicated transactions in order to disguise its origin from tax inspectors and the police; this is known as . . . . money.

    a. cleaning   b. laundering   c. washing

"*. . . so anyway, there we were in the outer office, and Pemberton was about to sign the chitty for me to get the XP90 requisition forms . . . you remember, they're the ones that authorise the throughput of interbranch communication data . . . when who should walk in bold as brass but Flaxton of Sales. 'Hullo,' I said, 'What are **you** doing in this neck of the woods?' 'Come and see J.J.,' he said. Now I know for a fact, and Freddy Robinson of Home Accounts can back me on this . . . that Flaxton is pushing for a promotion situation at Head Office, and that he's been muddying up **my** prospects in that area for some time. '**You're** a crafty so-and-so,' I joked casually, not letting him see how niggled I really was . . . when all of a sudden, the intercom buzzed . . .*"

Word Partnerships – Tax

EXERCISE 1

All the words below can be combined with *tax* or *taxation* in a two-word partnership (e.g. *tax accounting, progressive taxation*). Add *tax* and/or *taxation* before or after the following words:

1. . . . . accounting . . . .
2. . . . . allowance . . . .
3. . . . . authority . . . .
4. . . . . avoidance . . . .
5. . . . . consultant . . . .
6. . . . . corporation . . . .
7. . . . . deductible . . . .
8. . . . . direct . . . .
9. . . . . evasion . . . .
10. . . . . free . . . .
11. . . . . haven . . . .
12. . . . . income . . . .
13. . . . . indirect . . . .
14. . . . . inspector . . . .
15. . . . . loophole . . . .
16. . . . . loss . . . .
17. . . . . payer . . . .
18. . . . . progressive . . . .
19. . . . . rates . . . .
20. . . . . rebate . . . .
21. . . . . regressive . . . .
22. . . . . return . . . .
23. . . . . sales . . . .
24. . . . . shelter . . . .
25. . . . . withholding . . . .
26. . . . . year . . . .

EXERCISE 2

Now use the correct form of these verbs in the following sentences:

avoid	be liable	deduct	evade
levy	lower	pay	raise

1. If you inherit a lot of money, you . . . . for capital transfer tax.

2. In some countries, employers have to . . . . tax from your pay and . . . . it direct to the tax authorities, so employees have no possibility of . . . . income tax.

3. Some people hire expensive accountants to tell them how to . . . . taxes – legally, of course!

4. The government always tries to . . . . taxes in the year before elections.

5. The government has a huge deficit and is going to have to . . . . either the rate of VAT or income tax.

6. The government . . . . special taxes on petrol, alcohol and tobacco.

Economic Theories

Read the following text about classical economic theory, Keynesianism, and various forms of neo-classicism. Then study the exercises which follow:

The 18th and 19th century classical economists, most notably Adam Smith in *The Wealth of Nations* (1776), argued in favour of "làissez-faire" and insisted that natural forces such as individual self-interest and competition naturally determine prices and incomes. Theoretically, under perfect competition – i.e. in the absence of monopolies, oligopolies, externalities, and so on – wages and prices would be perfectly flexible. It was argued that a perfectly competitive economy would produce a general equilibrium. This in turn would lead to "allocative efficiency", the point at which all the resources of an economy are being fully and efficiently employed, so that no particular output can be increased unless another is reduced, and no-one can become better off without making someone else worse off.

Yet the great depression of the 1930s demonstrated that, at least in the short term, the market system does not automatically lead to full employment. If people are pessimistic about the future, they will save more money and consume less, leading to a fall in production and employment. John Maynard Keynes recommended governmental intervention in the economy, to counter the business cycle: an increase in government spending or a decrease in taxation during a recession, to stimulate the economy and increase output, investment, consumption and employment; and a decrease in government spending or an increase in taxation in a period of inflation. To the classical argument that in the long run economies tend to settle at a full employment equilibrium, Keynes replied that "in the long run, we are all dead."

If the post-war period was the era of Keynesianism, events after the 1973 oil crisis demonstrated that Keynes did not have all the answers, and the late 1970s and the 1980s saw the rise of various forms of neo-classicism, all of which agree that medium or long-term economic growth is damaged by short-term Keynesian or "stop-go" government policies to stabilize the economy.

The ultimate aim of Keynesian governmental intervention or "demand management" is full employment – when no involuntary unemployment exists. However, this is now widely considered to be impossible, and even undesirable, as it causes inflation to rise. Many economists now talk about "the natural rate of unemployment" which corresponds to optimal output, when upward and downward forces on prices and wages are in balance, so that inflation is stable. In the 1960s, it was believed that there was a "trade-off" or exchange between low unemployment and high but stable inflation. Yet the development, in the 1970s and 1980s, of "stagflation" – high unemployment or stagnation *and* persistent and rising inflation, seems to disprove this. It also became clear that in the long run, low unemployment, achieved by fiscal policies, results in rising inflation, because inertial inflation always rises after inevitable shocks. Since it is argued that attempts to force unemployment below its natural rate lead to accelerating inflation, the natural rate is also known as the non-accelerating-inflation rate of unemployment (or NAIRU).

In his *General Theory of Employment, Interest and Money* (1936), Keynes argued that people's economic expectations about the future were generally erratic and random, and could consequently be systematically wrong. In the 1970s, the Rational Expectations school, led by Robert Lucas and Thomas Sargent, began to argue that, on the contrary, people (or "economic agents") generally make rational choices according to the information available to them. For example, if people anticipate that the government will cut taxes or allow the money supply to grow or interest rates to fall, so as to boost employment and stimulate demand, they will plan and behave accordingly. Even before the government announces such measures, companies will plan price rises, and trade unions will demand higher pay. This means that predictable and systematic policies to stabilize the business cycle (e.g., monetary expansion and tax cuts) will instantly be compensated for and thus become ineffective. In other words, fiscal or monetary policy will only affect output and unemployment if it is unpredictable and comes as a surprise, in much the same way as only random news shocks stock market prices.

Monetarists such as Milton Friedman argue that the average levels of prices, wages and economic activity are determined by the quantity of money in circulation and its velocity of circulation, and that inflation is caused by excessive monetary growth. Other economists have used the same data to argue that it is increased business activity that causes the money supply to rise, and that the money supply follows prices, and not vice versa. Monetarists claim that Keynesian attempts to stabilize the business cycle only lead to rising prices and the crowding out of private investment, and that the business cycle, inflation and unemployment are the unintended results of misconceived government interventions and of exogenous variables. They insist that free markets and competition are efficient and should be allowed to operate with a minimum of governmental intervention. If money supply, rather than fiscal policy, is the major determinant of nominal GNP growth, the role of the government should be to ensure a fixed growth rate for the money supply.

"Supply-side" theorists agree with Keynesians that there is a role for economic policy, but they argue that it should focus on aggregate supply or potential output rather than on aggregate demand. They recommend boosting supply in a stagnant economy by lowering taxes on capital and business profits, which will lead to an increase in the supply of inputs, namely capital and labour.

EXERCISE 1
Label the following statements with the names of the economists whose ideas they describe:
Adam Smith   John Maynard Keynes   Milton Friedman   Robert Lucas
1. The government should intervene in the economy to counter the business cycle.
2. The cause of inflation is unnecessary monetary growth.
3. Planned governmental intervention is not effective as the market will anticipate it.
4. Prices and incomes will find their natural level in an economy which is powered by free enterprise and individualism.

EXERCISE 2
Match the following word partnerships, all of which occurred in the text:
1. perfect
2. general
3. allocative
4. full
5. governmental
6. rational
7. money
8. demand
9. fiscal
10. business

a. employment
b. management
c. cycle
d. equilibrium
e. policy
f. competition
g. efficiency
h. expectations
i. intervention
j. supply

1		2		3		4		5		6		7		8		9		10	

EXERCISE 3

Here is a summary of the text. Use the following to fill in the spaces:

anticipate	market	consume	classical	taxation
counter	flexible	inflationary	stabilize	aggregate

The (1) .... economists argued that individual self-interest and competition naturally determine prices and incomes. In a perfectly competitive market, wages and prices would be perfectly (2) .... , leading to a general equilibrium. Yet the Depression of the 1930's demonstrated that the (3) .... system does not automatically lead to full employment, because if people are worried about the future, they save more and (4) .... less, which leads to falls in production and employment. Keynes recommended governmental intervention in the economy, to (5) .... the business cycle – increase or decreases in (6) .... and/or government spending as necessary.

Yet the 'stagflation' of the 1970's demonstrated the limits of Keynesianism. Recent neo-classicists argue that short-term policies to (7) .... the economy damage medium or long-term economic growth, and that full employment is necessarily (8) .... Furthermore, Rational Expectations theorists argue that economic agents are able to (9) .... and counteract fiscal and monetary policies. Monetarists argue that inflation is caused by excessive monetary growth, so that the role of government is to ensure a fixed growth rate for the money supply. Supply-side theorists believe that economic policy should focus on (10) .... supply, eg, boosting a stagnant economy by lowering taxes on capital and business profits.

EXERCISE 4

Match up the following words into pairs of opposites:

1. cut
2. exogenous
3. expansion
4. flexible
5. individual
6. nominal
7. private
8. save
9. supply
10. wealth

a. collective
b. contraction
c. demand
d. endogenous
e. increase
f. poverty
g. public
h. real
i. rigid or fixed
j. spend

1		2		3		4		5		6		7		8		9		10	

EXERCISE 5

Make the following words negative by using one of the following prefixes:

de-   dis-   im-   in-   un-

1. .... accelerating
2. .... intended
3. .... prove
4. .... desirable
5. .... natural
6. .... stabilize

7. .... effective
8. .... perfect
9. .... stable
10. .... efficiency
11. .... predictable
12. .... voluntary

Income

Complete the text by using the following words:

cost	differentials	distribution	earn
income	inequality	profits	progressive
purchasing	rent	salary	standard

Money paid, usually weekly and often in cash, to a worker for work done is called a wage (or wages). A (1) .... is a regular payment made to an employee, usually by a bank transfer or cheque at the end of the month. A real wage is an actual wage deflated (divided) by the consumer price index; this gives the (2) .... power of an hour's work. Skilled work is usually rewarded by higher pay than unskilled work. Skills, knowledge and expertise acquired in education or special training are also known as human capital, and are usually remunerated. On the contrary, compensating (3) .... are often paid to persuade unskilled people to take dangerous, dirty, inconvenient or tedious jobs. Subsistence wages are the minimum amount needed to support a person's life. Fortunately, most people in industrial and post-industrial countries (4) .... rather more than this. If higher wages tempt people to work longer hours, this is known as the substitution effect. But after a certain point, higher wages mean that workers can afford to work fewer hours; this is the (5) .... effect.

The (6) .... of living is defined as the level of prosperity in terms of material or social benefits (which are related to income and wealth). The (7) .... of living is the amount of money that must be paid for food, housing, clothing, and so on.

In economics, unlike in marketing, (8) .... concerns the allocation of factors of production – land, which earns (9) ...., labour, which earns wages, and capital, which earns interest and/or profits – and their market prices. Income is the flow of money earned or collected during a given period, including wages and salaries, interest payments, rental income, and (10) .... from business. (11) .... or redistributive taxation can reduce income (12) .... Wealth is the net stock of tangible and financial assets owned at any particular time.

"If God had meant us to live within our means He wouldn't have given us credit cards!"

Pay

EXERCISE 1

Complete the text by using the following words:

bonus	**double time**	**golden handshake**	**incentive**
minimum wage	**overtime**	**pay differentials**	**pay scales**
pay-roll	**remuneration**	**salary**	**pension**
	time and a half	**wages**	

John Bright is the Marketing Director of MicroTech, a fast-growing electronic equipment manufacturer with 600 people on the (1) . . . . He was headhunted from another company, and his (2) . . . . is very high. He also gets a large annual (3) . . . . if sales are good, which is of course a big (4) . . . . to him. His predecessor was fired – but he was given a big (5) . . . .: approximately three years' (6) . . . ., plus a full (7) . . . ., even though he was only 58 years old.

MicroTech has a number of different (8) . . . . The cleaners do not earn much more than the (9) . . . . , and the production workers are paid according to their skill: there are strict (10) . . . . between fully-skilled and semi-skilled employees. The (11) . . . . of Paul Gascoigne, the janitor at the MicroTech headquarters, are not very high, but he has plenty of opportunities to do (12) . . . ., which earns him (13) . . . . in the evenings and on Saturdays, and (14) . . . . if he has to work on Sundays.

EXERCISE 2

Although pay is important there are, of course, many other aspects of work that people consider when choosing a job. Which of the following are important for you? Rank them in order of importance from 1 (most important) to 12 (least important) for you:

Variety of routine	. . . .
Responsibility for others	. . . .
Meeting people	. . . .
Power	. . . .
Working hours	. . . .
Working conditions	. . . .
Work atmosphere	. . . .
Holidays	. . . .
Opportunity to travel	. . . .
Job security	. . . .
Financial package	. . . .
Career opportunities	. . . .
Other	. . . .

If you are working in a group, compare your answers with another student.

Review – Opposites

Complete the sentences with a word that is (in an obvious sense) the opposite of one of the words in the box. If the word is a verb, you will need to use the appropriate form.

asset	credit	deposit	depreciate	endogenous
floating	privatize	retail	profit	trough

1. The bank seems to have . . . . my account by £100 by mistake.

2. I have to get to the bank before half past four to . . . . some money.

3. After the war, the French government . . . . all the major banks and insurance companies.

4. If things go on like this, we're going to make a huge . . . . at the end of the year.

5. Investors are beginning to worry that the business cycle will soon reach a . . . .

6. The government always claims that economic difficulties are the result of . . . . factors.

7. Until the beginning of the 1970s, we had a . . . . exchange rate.

8. Since the beginning of the year, the currency has . . . . by over 5%.

9. He likes his new job at the bank because now he's only dealing with . . . . business.

10. He's useless. He keeps making mistakes. In fact I'd say that he's a real . . . . to the department.

"The exercise bike was killing me."

Review – Economics 1

Classify the following 32 words into four groups of eight, according to these headings:

autarky	money supply
balance of payments	monopsony
barriers to entry	natural monopoly
barter	oligopsony
boom	peak
cartel	price level
comparative advantage	protectionism
cost-push	quotas
demand-pull	real GNP
depression	recession
downturn	slowdown
economies of scale	slump
excessive demand	spillovers
exports	tariffs
imperfect competition	trough
index-linked	wage/price spiral

Business Cycles	Competitive Theory	Inflation	International Trade
. . . .	. . . .	. . . .	. . . .
. . . .	. . . .	. . . .	. . . .
. . . .	. . . .	. . . .	. . . .
. . . .	. . . .	. . . .	. . . .
. . . .	. . . .	. . . .	. . . .
. . . .	. . . .	. . . .	. . . .
. . . .	. . . .	. . . .	. . . .
. . . .	. . . .	. . . .	. . . .

Review – Economics 2

In the wordbox below you should be able to find – horizontally (left to right), vertically (top to bottom), or diagonally (top left to bottom right) – 26 economic terms already seen in the previous pages.

```
S  T  A  G  F  L  A  T  I  O  N  D  I
T  U  J  Q  R  E  C  E  S  S  I  O  N
I  N  P  U  T  O  V  Y  C  R  O  W  D
M  G  N  P  X  Z  W  J  C  Q  U  N  E
U  E  M  P  L  O  Y  T  S  L  T  T  X
L  W  T  X  Z  Y  A  B  H  E  E  U  M
A  E  F  I  S  C  A  L  O  C  D  R  A
T  R  O  U  G  H  I  O  C  O  E  N  R
E  U  T  A  X  H  I  C  K  N  M  M  G
P  M  A  R  K  E  T  P  B  O  A  O  I
E  C  O  N  O  M  I  S  T  M  N  N  N
A  S  C  A  R  C  E  D  Y  I  D  E  A
K  E  Y  N  E  S  I  A  N  C  H  Y  L
```

Growth Metaphors

EXERCISE 1

A common metaphor in finance is that of growth – seeds are planted, grow, and flower.

Here are 15 words normally associated with farming. Put them in the appropriate spaces in the sentences below:

green	branching out	sprouted
flourishing	sowing	blossoming
reap	spreading	weed out
fertile	grew	roots
branches	fruit	ploughing

1. Throughout the recession, politicians talked about 'the . . . . shoots of recovery.'

2. Business is . . . . in the industrial north of the country.

3. Financial instruments seem to be a very . . . . area.

4. In the continuing hot weather, sales of electric fans are . . . .

5. Our success is the . . . . of many years of careful planning and market research.

6. Small micro-electronics companies suddenly . . . . all over the valley.

7. The entire company . . . . from one simple idea.

8. We believe that we are . . . . the seeds of profitable activities in the future.

9. We expect to . . . . very substantial rewards within a maximum of five years.

10. We're going to have to . . . . the less profitable items in the product line.

11. We're opening new . . . . at the rate of one a week.

12. We're . . . . most of the profits back into the business.

13. We've put down . . . . in Eastern Europe.

14. We've been rapidly . . . . onto the Continent.

15. Without neglecting our core business, we're . . . . into lots of new activities.

NOTE
Ploughing (GB) = plowing (US)

EXERCISE 2

In English, words related to UP usually have good and positive meanings, while words related to DOWN usually mean something negative.

Mark the following sentences +ve or –ve according to their meaning:

1. We hit a peak last year.
2. She really fell in status.
3. It's been downhill ever since.
4. The company is in tip-top shape.
5. That was a low trick.
6. We've boosted productivity.
7. We're sinking fast.
8. Our exports soared after the devaluation.
9. Things are at an all-time low.
10. Our sales rose in the last quarter.
11. My heart sank when I saw the balance sheet.
12. I'm feeling over the moon! I've finished!

Word Chains

Look at the following chain of words:

market   share   capital   investment   bank

Together these words make up a series of four word partnerships:

> **market share, share capital, capital investment, investment bank**

Rearrange the following groups of words so that they make up similar chains of word partnerships:

1. cost – net – opportunity – profit – accounting

2. department – maintenance – cost – marginal – price

3. index – capital – price – market – risk

4. tax – limited – loss – corporation – leader

5. retail – procedures – tax – sales – accounting

6. share – bull – linked – index – market

7. unearned – tax – enterprise – income – free

8. value – account – merchant – book – bank

Mini-Dictionary of Finance

A selective list of 1,000 common terms

"The definition of a recession is when your neighbor loses
his job – a depression is when you lose yours."
US President HARRY S. TRUMAN

Financial and Economic Terms

> Note: only one (financial) meaning is given for most words and terms; some words also have other, non-financial, meanings.

above par - describes a bond or other fixed-interest security whose market value is higher than the price at which it was issued

above the line - normal business expenses and revenues that come above the net income or net profit in a profit and loss account or income statement

absolute advantage - the ability to produce a particular good more cheaply than other countries

absorption costing - see **full costing**

accelerated depreciation - subtracting a high proportion of the cost of capital investments from taxable profit during the first years of use

accelerator or **acceleration principle** - changes in the demand for consumer goods cause even greater changes in the demand for capital goods

accepting houses - banks that buy (for a commission or fee) export merchants' short-term bills of exchange, expecting the debtor to pay up at the right time

account - a statement of money paid or owed; an arrangement with a firm that allows credit for payments

accountability - the state of being responsible to someone for some actions (company directors are **accountable** to the company's shareholders)

accountancy - the profession or business of an accountant

accountant - person who keeps and checks an organization's or an individual's financial records

account day or **settlement day** - the day on which all deals made during the previous 14-day **account** or **accounting period** on the London Stock Exchange must be settled

accounting - keeping financial records (recording income and expenditure, and profits and losses, valuing assets and liabilities, etc.)

accounting-entity assumption - see **separate-entity principle**

accounting-period assumption - see **time-period principle**

accounting equation - the fundamental identity of the balance sheet: Assets = Liabilities + Owners' Equity

accounting principles - a dozen or so concepts, conventions or doctrines generally observed in accounting

accounting standards - a country's exact rules concerning valuation, measurement and disclosure

accounts - a company's set of accounting records for a particular period

accounts payable - see **creditors**

accounts receivable - see **debtors**

accrual - a gradual or automatic increase in an amount of money (e.g. interest), usually money owed to someone; (**to accrue**)

accrual basis - in a budget or balance sheet, estimates expenses and income for the period in which they are incurred rather than actually spent or received

accrued expenses - expenses incurred at the date of the balance sheet, but not yet paid (e.g. wages, taxes and interest)

accrued revenue - revenue earned but not yet received or recorded

accumulate - to grow by way of regular additions (e.g. accumulated debts)

acid-test ratio - see **quick-asset ratio**

acquire - to buy, to gain, to get, to receive, to take possession of something; to take over a company by buying its shares; to make an **acquisition**

actuary - person who calculates probabilities for an insurance company, so that it can set its premiums

administrator - see **liquidator**

affiliate - one of a group of companies which is wholly or partly owned by another; to enter into association with others

114

agent - person who negotiates purchases and sales in return for commission or a fee

aggregate demand - the total amount spent in a country by consumers, companies and the government

aggregate supply - the amount of output that business produces and sells, given current prices, costs and production capacity

aid - money given to developing countries by richer ones

allocating costs - the process of assigning costs to individual products, processes and departments

allocative efficiency - the situation in which all the resources in an economy are fully and efficiently employed

amalgamate - to merge, to combine; to join two or more businesses into a single organization

amortization - the process of repaying a debt by instalments; in company accounts the systematic write-off of costs incurred to acquire an asset (to **amortize**)

Annual General Meeting (AGM) (GB) or **Annual Stockholders Meeting** (US) - a yearly meeting to which companies have to invite all shareholders

annual report - sent by all publicly quoted (US: listed) companies to their shareholders after each financial year (before the AGM)

annuity insurance - a life assurance contract in which the insurer pays a fixed sum of money annually, usually in return for a single cash premium

annuity system of depreciation - spreads the cost of an asset equally over several years and charges this, and an amount representing the interest on current value, each year

anti-trust laws - legislation (especially in the US) to prevent commercial and industrial companies forming large, potentially monopolistic combinations

appreciate - to increase in price or value

appreciation - an increase in the value of an asset

arbitrage - the simultaneous buying and selling of the same currency in different markets to profit from rate differentials

arbitrageur - person who buys and sells currencies for profit; a person who buys stakes in companies involved (or expected to be involved) in takeover bids

arrears - money owed that should already have been paid, e.g. rent, taxes, subscriptions, etc.

Articles of Association (GB) or **Bylaws** (US) - the rules and regulations of a company, setting out shareholders' rights, directors' duties, etc.

artificial person - a company or corporation, which according to law has an existence separate from the actual persons who run and own it

asset - anything of value owned by a business that can be used to produce goods, pay liabilities, etc.; often used in the plural - **assets**

asset-stripping - buying a poorly performing or under-valued company and then selling off the assets at a profit

asset turnover - the ratio of a company's net sales to its average assets

asset value per share - the total book-value of all a company's assets divided by the number of ordinary shares issued

assurance - contract guaranteeing payment of a fixed sum upon the occurrence of a specified event (typically, **life assurance**, with the sum payable on death or retirement)

auction - (verb and noun) a way of selling at a public meeting in which each item is sold to whoever makes the highest bid

audit - (verb and noun) an inspection (or check for accuracy) and an evaluation of financial records by a second set of accountants (called **auditors**)

audit report - written by the external auditors, declares that the annual financial statements present a true and fair view or a fair presentation of the company's situation

austerity - economic situation when policies designed to reduce inflation, imports, government spending, etc. are in operation

autarky - total self-sufficiency and the consequent absence of foreign trade

authorized share capital (GB) or **authorized capital stock** (US) - the maximum amount of a particular type of share a company can issue, as stipulated in the Memorandum of Association (or Certificate of Incorporation)

available assets - see **liquid assets**

average cost - the sum of variable and fixed costs divided by the number of units produced

backward integration - when a company takes over or acquires its suppliers of raw materials or components

bad debts - amounts of debtors (GB) or accounts receivable (US) that are never likely to be paid

bail out - to rescue a person or organization in financial difficulties by providing money

balance - the amount of money (or the size of the deficit) in an account at a particular time; an amount of money remaining to be paid

balance of payments - the difference between what a country pays for its imports and receives for its exports

balance of trade - the difference between the money values of a country's visible imports and exports

balance sheet - financial statement which shows a company's financial condition (amount of debits and credits) on the last day of an accounting period

bank - (verb) to have an account with a bank

bank account - an arrangement with a bank to deposit and withdraw money, settle bills, etc.

banker's draft - a document guaranteeing payment by a bank (often used instead of cheques to pay bills in foreign currencies)

banker's order - see **standing order**

Bank for International Settlements (BIS) - the central bankers' central bank in Basle

bank holiday - in Britain, public holidays (Christmas, Easter, etc.); in the US, when the government temporarily closes a bank to prevent panic (a run on the bank)

bank loan - a fixed sum of money, lent for a fixed period, on which interest is paid

banknote - a piece of paper money, issued by a (central) bank

bankruptcy - the state of being bankrupt or insolvent: unable to pay debts

bank statement - a record of all transactions (credits and debits) in a bank account during a particular period

barometer stock (GB) or **bellwether stock** (US) - a widely-held stock that can be considered as an indicator of present and future market performance

barriers to entry - factors which prevent or deter new producers from entering an industry

barter or **counter-trade** - the exchange of one good for another, without the use of money

base rate (GB) or **prime rate** (US) - the lowest lending rate, which banks charge blue chip borrowers

basket of currencies - a weighted average of a selection of different currencies used by the IMF for Special Drawing Rights

bear - (verb) to support or carry a risk, a responsibility, etc.

bear - a person who sells shares hoping to buy them back at a lower price before the next account or settlement day

bearer share - a share made out to whoever possesses it, without the owner's name being written on it

bear market - a period during which stock market or currency prices are falling

bear spread - an options strategy designed to profit from a fall in the price of a security or commodity

bellwether stock - see **barometer stock**

below par - describes a bond or other fixed interest security whose market value is lower than its face value

below the line - extraordinary items placed below the net profit figure in a profit and loss account or income statement

bid - (to make) an offer to buy something at a particular price

Big Bang - in October 1986, abolished minimum brokers' commissions and introduced new electronic dealing systems at the London Stock Exchange

bill - a statement of money owed for goods or services; (US) a banknote

bill of exchange or **commercial bill** - a written order instructing someone (usually an importer) to pay someone else (usually an exporter) a certain sum on a given date

bill of lading - document giving title to goods that acts as a receipt and a contract to ship them, and can be used by shippers as security when discounting bills of exchange

black market - goods or currencies sold illegally

blue chip - a security in a company considered to be virtually without risk

bond - an interest-bearing security, redeemed after a fixed period

bonus - something extra, usually a payment, as a reward for good work, or for undertaking a dangerous or unpleasant job

bonus issue or **scrip issue** or **capitalization issue** - British names for new shares issued to shareholders instead of a dividend

bookkeeping or **book-keeping** - recording financial data by writing down the details of transactions

book value - the worth of an asset as recorded in a company's accounts

boom - a period when demand is rising, and an economy is working close to capacity

boost (an economy) - to expand it by fiscal policies: increased government spending or decreased taxation

borrow - to receive money that will later have to be paid back (usually plus interest)

bottom line - the net profit or net income line on a profit and loss account or income statement

bought deal - an arrangement by which a merchant bank or investment bank finds buyers for bonds before they are even offered for sale

branch - a local office or shop of a business

breakdown - an analysis or classification of something (e.g. costs) into component parts

breakeven point - sales volume at which a company covers its costs

Bretton Woods Agreement - pegged or fixed the value of many currencies against the US$, which was pegged against the price of gold (1944-1971)

bridging loan (GB) or **bridge loan** (US) - a loan for a short period, covering the time between needing to spend money and receiving money that is due

broker - an agent in a particular market, such as securities, commodities, insurance, etc.

bubble - a period during which speculative investors buy shares, pushing their prices up to unsustainable levels

budget - a financial operating plan showing expected income and expenditure

building society - an organization (in Britain) that receives deposits and lends money as mortgages to home-buyers

bull - person who buys securities expecting their price to rise so that he or she can resell them before the next account day

bullion - gold bars (or silver or other precious metals), often part of banks' reserves

bull market - a period during which stock market or currency prices are rising

bull spread - an option strategy that speculates on a rise in the price of a security or commodity

burden rate - the rate at which indirect costs are allocated to specific products, processes or departments

business - trade and commerce in general; or an organization that makes or buys and sells goods or provides a service

business market - see **industrial market**

buyout - see **leveraged buyout and management buyout**

Bylaws - see **Articles of Association**

calendar spread - involves buying and selling options on the same security with different maturities

called-up capital - the amount of money a company has when shareholders have only paid for part of the total share capital that has been issued

call option - the right to buy a fixed quantity of a commodity, security or currency at a certain price on a certain future date

cambist - a dealer in foreign currencies and bills of exchange

cap or **ceiling** - the upper limit of a floating interest rate

capital - the money invested in a business and used to buy the assets

capital allowance - the amount of tax-free profit allowed to cover the cost of replacing fixed assets

capital assets - see **fixed assets**

capital formation or **accumulation** - spending money to increase the supply of capital goods rather than consumer goods

capital gains tax - a tax on profits from the sale of assets

capital goods or **investment goods** - goods that are used to make further goods; the goods that make up the industrial market (machines, tools, factories, etc.)

capital intensive - requiring a large amount of capital investment per employee

capital market - the banks and financial institutions from which companies and governments can raise long term finance

capital ratio - is between a bank's capital and reserves on the one hand, and its total assets (loans) on the other

capital sum - a lump sum of money paid by an insurance company (after an accident, on retirement, etc.)

capital transfer tax - see **inheritance tax**

capital turnover ratio - the ratio of annual sales to issued share-capital

capitalism - economic system based on the private ownership of the means of production, distribution and exchange

capitalization - the aggregate stock market price of all a company's ordinary shares or common stock

capitalization issue - see **bonus issue**

carrying cost - the cost of owning assets, which can be compared with the amount of interest that could be earned if the money was lent instead

cartel - a group of producers or sellers who combine to avoid competition and increase profits by fixing prices and quantities

cash - money in the form of banknotes and coins

cashcard - a plastic card issued by a bank to its customers to use in cash dispensers

cash discount - a price reduction offered for immediate cash payment

cash dispenser - a computerized machine that allows bank customers to withdraw money, check their balance, etc., by using their cashcard and a private number, called a PIN number

cash flow - a company's ability to earn cash; the amount of cash made during a specified period which can be used for investment

ceiling - see **cap**

central bank - the bank that issues currency, carries out the government's financial policy, etc.

certificate of deposit - short-term, interest-bearing bank deposits that can be traded like a share or bond

Certificate of Incorporation - see **Memorandum of Association**

Certified Public Accountant (CPA) - person who has passed the standard American accounting examinations

Chartered Accountant - person who has passed the standard British accounting examinations

checking account - see **current account**

cheque (GB) or **check** (US) - a written order to a bank to pay on demand a specified sum to a named person or business

cheque card - a plastic card issued by a bank guaranteeing cheques drawn on the customer's account, up to a certain limit

circulating assets - see **current assets**

City (the) - collective name for all the financial institutions in London

claim - demand made to an insurance company for payment according to an insurance policy; a demand for higher wages, etc.; to make such a demand

classical unemployment - the loss of jobs caused when wages are too high

clean floating exchange rate - see **freely floating**

clear - (adjective) describes a market situation in which prices fluctuate until supply matches demand; (verb) to pass a cheque through the banking system

clearing - the process by which cheques and other payments are passed through the banking system

closing entry - a journal entry transferring a balance from an ongoing account to the profit and loss account at the end of an accounting period

collar - a double limit to a floating interest rate, comprising both a floor and a ceiling (lower and upper limits)

collateral - anything that acts as a security or a guarantee for a loan

collective bargaining - group negotiations between trade unions and employers, concerning pay and working conditions

collectivism - economic system in which the means of production are owned by the state, which plans the economy, sets prices and output levels, etc.

command economy - see **planned economy**

commerce - the buying and selling of goods and the activities of banks and other financial institutions

commercial bank - a business that trades in money, receiving and holding deposits, paying money according to customers' instructions, lending money, etc.

commercial bill - see **bill of exchange**

commercial paper - short-term, discounted and unsecured corporate debt of large American banks and companies issued as a way of borrowing money

commercial traveller or **(US) traveling salesman** - alternative names for a sales representative

commission - money paid to sales representatives, proportional to the total value of the goods they sell; money charged by a bank for undertaking a transaction

commodities - either goods in general, or specific raw materials or primary products (cereals, metals, tea, coffee, rubber, etc.) traded on special markets

common pricing - an agreement between companies to sell at the same prices, or to tender at the same price

common stock - see **ordinary shares**

company or corporation (US) - an association of people formally registered as a business (partnership, limited company, etc.)

comparative advantage or **comparative cost principle** - relative advantage in the production of particular goods over some, but not all, other countries

compensation - money paid (by an insurer) to someone who has suffered injury or had property lost or damaged

competition - rivalry between businesses in the same market

competitive advantage - the element that makes one company better than its competitors: a better product or service, lower prices (due to economies of scale), etc.

competitive bidding - see **tendering**

competitor - a rival in business offering the same or similar goods or services

component - any of the pieces or parts that make up a machine, product, etc.

conglomerate - a large corporation, or a group of companies, marketing a large number of different goods or services

conservatism or **prudence** - an accounting principle which states that where alternative accounting methods are possible, one understates rather than overstates profits

consistency principle - the same methods (of inventory valuation, depreciation, etc.) are used from one accounting period to the next

consolidated statements - the combination of the financial statements of a parent company and its subsidiaries, as if they formed a single entity

consumer or **end-use**r - person who (buys and) uses goods or services; person whose needs are satisfied by producers

consumer goods - goods that are bought and used by the public, rather than being used for manufacturing further goods

consumer market - the individuals and households that buy products for their own personal consumption

consumer price index - see **retail price index**

consumption - the using, or using up of goods

consumption function - the relation between the level of consumption and the level of consumers' disposable income

contingent liabilities - possible future liabilities that are mentioned in notes added to a balance sheet

continuity principle or **going-concern assumption** - in accounting, assumes that a business will continue indefinitely into the future

contract - a legal agreement, e.g. to buy, to sell, to provide insurance, etc.; or to shrink or get smaller

contraction - act of getting smaller, like national income during a recession

controlling interest - possession of more than 50% of a company's voting shares, allowing one to decide policy

convertible bond - fixed interest company security which the holder may convert into the issuer's ordinary shares at a specified price

convertible currency - one that can be freely exchanged for others

corporation tax - the tax on company profits in Britain

correspondent bank - one that works as an agent for another bank, especially abroad

cost accounting - involves the determination of the unit cost of a particular product made by a company, including materials, labour, overheads, etc.

cost leadership - a strategy that aims to create a competitive advantage by producing goods at a lower cost than competitors

cost of living - the amount of money that has to be paid for essentials such as food, accommodation, heating, clothing, etc.

cost-plus pricing or **mark-up pricing** - involves adding a fixed percentage to unit cost (which includes an approximate allocation of fixed costs)

cost-push inflation - when costs (rather than excessive demand) push up prices and wages (e.g. excessive wage increases or increases in the price of oil)

counter-trade - see **barter**

coupon - the amount of interest paid by a bond

crash - a dramatic collapse in the value of stocks and shares, caused by large-scale selling

creative accounting or **window dressing** - the attempt to disguise the true financial position of a company

credit - an arrangement to receive goods or services but pay later; an amount of money paid into a bank account; an amount entered on the right-hand side of an account, recording a payment received; to make such an entry

credit card - a plastic card issued by a bank or finance company that guarantees payment for goods or services purchased by the cardholder, who pays back the bank at a later date

creditor - person or organization to whom money is owed (for goods or services rendered, or as repayment of a loan)

creditors (GB) or **accounts payable** (US) - on a balance sheet, money a business owes to suppliers for purchases made on credit

credit standing or **credit rating** or **creditworthiness** - a lender's estimation of a borrower's present and future solvency

credit terms - the possibility of paying for goods in instalments, over a period of time

crowding in - theory that government borrowing and expenditure can lead to higher economic activity and a subsequent increase in private investment

crowding out - the fact that borrowing money for public investment reduces the amount of money available for private investment

cum div - means that the shareholder will receive the next dividend payment

currency - the money used in a particular country

currency swap - an exchange of one currency for another between two borrowers in different countries

current account (GB) or **checking account** (US) - bank account which pays no or little interest, but allows the holder to withdraw his or her cash with no restrictions

current assets or **circulating assets** or **floating assets** - those which will be consumed or turned into cash in the ordinary course of business

current cost accounting or **replacement cost accounting** - values assets (and related expenses like depreciation) at the price that would have to be paid to replace them today

current liabilities or **current debt** - are usually (arbitrarily) defined as debts to be paid within one year of the date of the financial statement

current ratio or **working capital ratio** - measures liquidity, and is current assets divided by current liabilities

current revenue pricing - maximizing current (short-term) sales revenue

current value - the actual value of an asset, as opposed to its historical price

current yield - the income from a security expressed as a percentage of its present market price

customer - person (or company) that buys a product or service from a shop or a producer

customs duties - taxes charged on most imports (except in customs unions or free trade areas like the European Union and NAFTA)

cyclical surplus or **deficit** - is caused by the business cycle (e.g. changes in tax revenues), rather than by deliberate government policy

cyclical unemployment - occurs during recessions, when the demand for labour declines

dawn raid - an attempt to acquire a large number of a company's shares by buying through several brokers just as the market opens

deal - an agreement to buy or sell goods or provide a service; to trade (buy or sell) something, e.g. securities, foreign currencies

dealer - a person who buys and resells merchandise or services to make a profit

debenture - a fixed interest loan issued by a company and (in Britain) secured by its assets

debit - an amount entered on the left-hand (debtor) side of an account; to make such an entry

debt - (pronounced /det/) money owed to someone (for a business this might include bank loans, debentures, bonds, bills for goods or services, etc.)

debt financing - the issuing of bonds, debentures, etc., that have to be repaid

debt/equity ratio - the amount of money a company has borrowed divided by shareholders' equity

debtor - person, company or country that has borrowed money

debtors (GB) or **accounts receivable** (US) - sums of money owed by customers for goods or services purchased on credit

declining balance method of depreciation - see **reducing balance method**

deduct - to take away an amount of something (e.g. a withholding tax deducted from share dividends)

default - to fail to repay a loan at the scheduled time, or to fail to respect a contract

defensive shares - offer a good yield but only a limited chance of a rise or decline in price

defer - to put off (a payment, a decision, etc.) to a later time

deferred liabilities - money owed that will not have to be paid during the current year: long-term loans, debentures, mortgages, etc.

deferred shares - do not receive a dividend until other categories of shares have received theirs

deficit - a deficiency, or an excess of expenditure over income

deflation - the opposite of inflation, a reduction in the money supply

del credere agent - an agent who bears the risk of non-payment by his customers; for taking this risk he or she is usually paid an extra commission

demand - the willingness and ability of consumers to purchase goods and services; to ask for something forcefully

demand-differential pricing or **multiple pricing** - selling the same good or service at different prices to different market segments

demand management - the Keynesian policy of stimulating an economy in a period of recession, and contracting it if it overheats

demand-pull inflation - rising prices caused when total demand exceeds what a country can produce, even at full employment

demerge - to split up a previously merged company into separate businesses once again

de-nationalize - see **privatize**

deposit - to place money in a bank; an amount of money in a bank; an amount of money paid to reserve an item; an amount of money paid when hiring something (e.g. a car) that is repaid if it is returned in good condition

deposit account - pays interest, but usually cannot be used for paying cheques (US: checks); notice is often required to withdraw money

depreciate - to lose value, or decline in price

depreciation - the reduction in value of a fixed asset due to use, obsolescence, etc. (by a charge against profits); or the loss of value of a currency

depression - a serious, long-lasting recession, as in the early 1930s

deregulation - the ending or relaxing of legal regulations or restrictions in a particular industry (e.g. the stock exchanges in New York in 1975, in London in 1986)

derivatives - financial instruments such as options that are based on underlying securities

derived demand - secondary demand: e.g. the demand for industrial goods which itself depends on the demand for consumer goods

devaluation - when a government or central bank formally decreases the value of its currency under a system of otherwise fixed exchange rates

diminishing balance method of depreciation - see **reducing balance method**

direct cost - see **prime cost**

direct costing or **variable costing** - provides the average variable cost for a product or process (which often depends on the volume manufactured)

direct debit - like a **standing order**, but the amount is not specified in advance

direct selling - when manufacturers sell directly to retailers, without using wholesalers; or when wholesalers sell directly to the public without using retailers

direct taxes - are levied on people's incomes and companies' profits

dirty floating exchange rate - see **managed floating**

discount - a price reduction; to sell at a reduced price, in return for the purchase of a large quantity, payment in cash, rapid payment, etc.; or to sell a bill at below its face value

discount broker - stockbroker who buys and sells for customers, but offers no investment advice, and therefore charges low commissions

discounted cash flow - a method of calculating how profitable an investment will be, by looking at the amount paid, the interest earned, and the degree of risk taken

discount houses - banks in London that buy (at a discount) and resell both traders' bills of exchange and short-term government securities

discount rate - the interest rate at which central banks discount government and other sure debt instruments from commercial banks; the rate at which they lend to commercial banks with such instruments as collateral

disinflation - government policy designed to slow down price inflation

disposable income - the amount of money that a person has left after paying taxes, compulsory insurance contributions, etc.

distribution - in economics, refers to the division of a community's income among its members; in marketing, moving goods to outlets where they are sold

distribution channel - all the companies or individuals involved in moving a particular good or service from the producer to the final consumer

distributor - person or organisation that stocks and resells components or goods to manufacturers or retailers

diversification - moving into new markets or activities so as to reduce or spread risks, often by buying other companies in different fields

divest - to sell assets or subsidiary companies

dividend - a share in the annual profits of a limited company, paid to shareholders

dividend payout ratio - expresses the percentage of income paid out to shareholders

domestic - of or inside a particular country (in economics); of or inside the home

double-entry bookkeeping - records the dual effect of every transaction: a value both received and paid

double time - double pay received for working overtime, usually on Sundays and public holidays

downturn - the end of a boom, when an economy starts to contract

drawing rights - loans in foreign currencies that come from the quota a country has contributed to the International Monetary Fund

dual currency bonds - are denominated in, and pay interest in, one currency, but are ultimately redeemed in another

dumping - selling goods in foreign markets at a lower price than in the home market, or even selling at cost price or at a loss in order to obtain foreign exchange

duty-free - describes goods that can be imported without customs taxes

earned income - money received for work (wages, salary, profits from one's business, royalties, pensions, etc.) rather than from investments or property

earnings - see **income**

earnings per share (EPS) - a company's distributable profit divided by the number of shares

earnings yield - (of a company), the proportion of total profits available for distribution to the total market value of the ordinary shares; (of a security), the last dividend paid as a percentage of the current market price

econometrics - the application of mathematical and statistical models to economic theories and problems

economic (adjective) - of or relating to an economy or economics

economical (adjective) - using a minimum of resources; or cheap

economic goods - those that are useful, scarce, and rationed by price

economic growth - an increase in per capita income, resulting from the increased production of goods and services

economic rent - money paid to someone over and above the amount he or she needs to remain in that particular line of work

economies of scale - reductions in unit costs arising from large-scale production

economies of scope - the cost advantages for an established manufacturer to make related products

economy - an organized system for the production, distribution and consumption of goods

efficiency - the ability to produce good results without wasting time or resources; in financial theory, the fact that all new information is rapidly communicated, understood by market participants, and incorporated into prices

elasticity of demand - the responsiveness of the quantity of a good or service demanded to changes in market price

elasticity of supply - changes in the supply of a good or service in response to changes in price

employ - to use somebody's labour or services in exchange for money

employee - person employed by someone else, working for money (salary or wages)

employer - person or organization who employs people who work for money

employment - the state of being employed, having paid work to do

endogenous - coming from or controlled from within, e.g. variables that are totally under the control of a company or a government

end-user - see **consumer**

enterprise - an informal term for a business organization; and the act of taking risks and setting up businesses

entrepreneur - person who organizes, finances and manages a business that produces and sells goods or services

equilibrium - a state of balance, such as when supply meets demand

equity financing - involves issuing stock or shares (equities) that will normally pay dividends but need never be repaid

Eurocurrency - any currency held outside its country of origin, bought and sold on Euromarkets (typically, the Yen, the Dollar, the Swiss Franc and the Deutschmark)

ex div - means that a shareholder buying the share now will not receive the next dividend payment

exchange controls - limits on the amount of a country's currency that residents can exchange for another

exchange rate - the price at which one currency can be exchanged for another one

Exchange Rate Mechanism - the part of the **European Monetary System** that limits fluctuations in exchange rates

excise duties - taxes raised on certain products, particularly tobacco and alcoholic drinks

exercise price or **strike price** of an option - the price at which the holder may buy or sell the underlying security

exogenous - coming from or controlled from without; uncontrollable variables

expansion - act of getting bigger, like an economy during a boom

export - to sell goods or services to another country; something sold to another country

external audit - a review of financial statements and accounting records by an accountant not belonging to the firm

externalities - costs imposed on others without their receiving compensation, or benefits received by others without their paying the proper costs

Extraordinary General Meeting (EGM) - a meeting that a company's directors may call if they need to consult shareholders over matters that cannot wait for the next AGM

face value - see **nominal value**

factoring - selling debts or receivables at a discount to someone who will try to collect the debt at full value

factors of production or **inputs** - resources used by firms in their production processes, namely land (and the natural resources in it), labour and capital

factory cost - prime cost (direct material and labour costs) plus overhead (US) or overheads (GB)

fair presentation - what American law requires accounts of a company's financial position to give

Federal Reserve Board ("The Fed") - the US central bank, made up of a group of twelve regional banks

fee or **fees** - money paid to accountants, lawyers, architects, private schools, etc.

fiduciary note issue - paper money (banknotes) that is not backed by reserves of gold

file for chapter 11 - in the US, to propose a recovery plan and be temporarily protected from creditors and given time to attempt to solve problems

final goods - goods that have been completed and are ready for sale

finance - funds and their provision and management; to provide funds

finance houses - institutions that lend money, at a high interest rate, for hire purchase or instalment credit

financial instruments - all the different ways of raising money, including bonds, shares, warrants, etc.

financial statements - the balance sheet, the profit and loss account (or income statement), the funds flow statement, etc.

financial supermarket - the name given to financial conglomerates arising from recent deregulation in the US and Britain

firm - another word for a partnership or other business

first-in, first-out (FIFO) - method of inventory valuation that assumes that the goods received first are sold first

fiscal - relating to government finances (taxation, expenditure, etc.)

fiscal year - an arbitrarily chosen 12-month period for tax purposes

Fisher equation - $MV = PT$, where M is money supply, V its velocity of circulation, P the price level, and T the volume of transactions

fixed assets or **capital assets** or **permanent assets** - items such as land, buildings, machines, etc., belonging to a business, which are expected to last for a long time, and cannot be sold or turned into cash, as they are used for making and selling the firm's products

fixed costs - those which do not vary according to the volume produced

fixed exchange rate - a rate that cannot change, whatever the pressures of supply and demand

flat yield or **running yield** - the amount of interest received from an investment expressed as a percentage of the price paid, disregarding any profit or loss made at redemption

flexible - (of prices, etc.) able to change according to supply and demand

float (a company) - to issue shares (offer them for sale to the public) for the first time (a **flotation**)

floating - (used for exchange rates, interest rates, etc.) able to change according to supply and demand

floating assets - see **current assets**

floating (or variable) rate note - a bond that pays interest according to current market rates

floor - the lower limit of a floating interest rate

flow of funds - cash received and payments made by a company during a specific period

fluctuate - (of numbers) to go up and down, rise and fall (the noun is **fluctuation**)

Footsie - popular name for the Financial Times-Stock Exchange (FT-SE) 100 Share Index, recording the average value of the 100 leading British shares

foreign exchange - currency of countries other than one's own

forward integration - consists of a company acquiring control of its distribution systems

forward market - over-the-counter futures deals for non-standardized quantities or time periods, e.g. for currencies

founders - the people who set up or establish a company

franchise - a licence giving someone an exclusive right to manufacture or sell certain products in a certain area; (the person who sells the licence is the **franchiser**; the person who buys it is the **franchisee**)

fraud - deceiving someone to obtain goods or money dishonestly

free enterprise - economic system in which anyone can attempt to raise capital, form a business, and offer goods or services

freely floating or **clean floating exchange rate** - one that is determined entirely by supply and demand

free market - one in which prices rise and fall according to supply and demand, with no governmental intervention

free trade - situation where there are no restrictions (tariffs, quotas, etc.) on imports and exports of goods

freeze - a fixing of prices, wages, rents, etc. at current levels

frictional unemployment - temporary unemployment that arises when people voluntarily leave a job to look for another one

friendly takeover - a takeover which is not contested by a company's board of directors

FT Index - or the Financial Times Ordinary Share Index, is based on 30 leading industrial and commercial shares

FT-SE 100 Share Index - see **Footsie**

full costing or **absorption costing** - the allocation of all fixed and variable costs relating to production in the calculation of the price of goods or services

full employment - the situation in which everyone looking for work is able to find it

full-disclosure principle - requires that financial reporting should include all significant information

fund - to provide money for a specific purpose; an amount of money saved for a specific purpose

funds - see **working capital**

funds flow statement or **source and application of funds** - a statement of changes in financial position detailing the causes of flows of resources into and out of a company

futures contract - an arrangement to buy or sell a commodity or currency or financial instrument at an agreed price at a future date

futures market - a market in which futures contracts for certain commodities are agreed

galloping inflation - inflation in two or three digits (e.g. 30, 60 or 100%)

GATT - General Agreement on Tariffs and Trade, designed to reduce protectionism and increase international trade, succeeded in 1994 by the World Trade Organization

gearing or **leverage** or **proprietary ratio** - the ratio between a company's share capital and its debt (bonds, debentures, bank loans)

general equilibrium - a hypothetical state of balance in all the markets which make up an economy (supply and demand of goods, labour, capital, etc.)

gilts or **gilt-edged stock** - long-term bonds issued by the British government

Glass-Steagall Act - in the US (like "Article 65" in Japan) enforced a strict separation between commercial banks and investment banks or stockbroking firms

GNP (gross national product) - the money value of all the final goods and services produced in a country in a year, plus income from foreign investments (which is excluded in **GDP** or **gross domestic product**)

GNP gap - the difference between real and potential GNP, if the economy is working at less than full employment (or the "natural rate of employment")

going-concern assumption - see **continuity principle**

going rate pricing - following the lead of competitors and setting the same price as them

golden handcuffs - large payments (e.g. in the form of a low interest loan) made to important employees to prevent them leaving the company

golden handshake - large sum of money paid as compensation to someone who is obliged to leave a job or retire early

golden parachute - an agreement to pay a large sum of money to senior employees if they lose their jobs, for example after a takeover

gold standard or **gold convertibility** - a system whereby a currency could be exchanged for a fixed amount of gold (until the 1970s)

goods on hand - see **merchandise inventory**

goodwill - the value to an established firm of its loyal customers, skilled staff and management; the value of a firm above its net asset value

greenmail - blackmail by way of dollars ("greenbacks"); buying a stake in a company, threatening to take it over, and then offering to sell the shares back at a profit

gross profit - net profit before depreciation and interest are deducted

gross yield of an investment - the percentage return before income tax is paid

growth - getting bigger, by increasing sales or markets, or acquiring other companies, etc.

growth share or **stock** - one that is expected to appreciate in capital value

hard currency - currency of a country with a strong balance of payments, which is unlikely to lose value in the near future

hedging - reducing the risk of unfavourable movement in commodity or security prices, or exchange or interest rates, by way of futures contracts

hidden reserves - arise when there is a considerable difference between the book value and the market value of assets

High Street banks - common British name for the commercial banks with large numbers of branches all over the country

higher - adjective meaning greater, larger: e.g. higher prices; (cannot be used as a verb, instead use **raise**)

hire purchase or **instalment credit** - loans to consumers that are repaid over 2 or 3 years

historical cost accounting - records the original price paid for goods (minus accumulated depreciation charges), rather than their current or replacement value

hive off - to sub-contract, or to separate part of a business, to make it a subsidiary

holding or **stake** - the amount of a person's (or organization's) financial investment in a business

holding company - a company that owns more than 50% of the capital of other companies which it therefore controls

honour - to accept or pay a cheque or bill of exchange when it becomes due

horizontal integration - mergers or takeovers among companies producing the same type of goods or services

hostile takeover - one which does not have the backing of a company's board of directors

hot money - money that is transferred from country to country to take advantage of higher interest and exchange rates

human capital - another name for labour (specifically, the skills and abilities of trained or educated workers)

hyperinflation - inflation of several hundred or thousand per cent (e.g. in Germany in the 1920s, Serbia and Russia in the 1990s, etc.)

illiquid assets - those that cannot be converted into money at short notice

imperfect competition - situations in which goods are priced too highly because of lack of competition (monopolies, oligopolies, etc.) or lack of information about market conditions

import - to buy goods or services from another country; something bought from another country

import substitution - the attempt to reduce imports by producing goods domestically

in-the-money - call options with an exercise price below the underlying share's current market price; put options with an exercise price above the share's market price

income or **revenue** or **earnings** - all the money received by a person or company during a given period (wages, salaries, rent, business profits, dividends, etc.)

income effect of higher prices - when the price of a necessary good rises, consumers' real income and spending on all goods falls

income effect of higher wages - if people earn more they can afford to work fewer hours (and have more time to spend their money)

income statement - the American name for the financial statement which shows the profit or loss made by a company during the accounting period

income tax - tax on people's income, and also on business profits in the US

income velocity of the circulation of money - the number of times a unit of money forms part of someone's income during a given period (GNP divided by the money supply)

incoterms - internationally accepted terms concerning transport and insurance costs used in international trade contracts

Incorporated - a word added to the name of a US company, signifying that it is a corporation with limited liability

increment - an increase, e.g. an annual rise in a salary

indebtedness - the condition of owing money

indemnify - to compensate someone for loss or injury, etc.

index-linked - (of a wage, salary, pension, tax, etc.) automatically raised to compensate for inflation, on the basis of an official price index

indirect taxes - those levied on the sale of goods and services

industrial market or **producer market** or **business market** - all the people or organizations that buy goods and services used in the production or supply of other goods or services

inefficient - not working in the best way, so that time or money or other resources are wasted

inelastic - (of supply and demand) unresponsive to changes in price

inflation - a rise in the general level of prices, and an increase in the money supply

inflationary - causing inflation

inflation rate - the percentage amount that prices (e.g. the retail price index) are higher than a year previously

infrastructure - services such as roads, railways, electricity, telephones, etc.

inheritance tax or **capital transfer tax** - a tax on gifts and inheritances

innovation - the development of new products, services, etc.

inputs - see **factors of production**

insider - person who occupies a position of trust within a company and possesses information not known to the public

insider dealing - buying or selling shares when in possession of privileged information that affects the price (e.g. while working for the company or an investment bank)

insolvent - (adjective) unable to pay debts (the noun is **insolvency**)

instalments - regular part payments of debts, etc.

instalment credit - see **hire purchase**

institutional investors - pension funds, insurance companies, investment trusts, etc., which hold a large proportion of the shares of leading companies

insurance - the provision of financial protection for property, life, health, etc. against specified risks (accident, fire, theft, loss, damage, death, etc.)

insurance agent - person who sells insurance policies, for a single insurance company, in return for a commission

insurance broker - a middleman or agent who negotiates insurance contracts for customers, using different companies

insurance policy - a contract between a customer and an insurance company, which will pay for particular losses or damage in return for one or more payments, known as premiums

intangible assets - those whose value can only be quantified or turned into cash with difficulty (e.g. goodwill, patents, copyrights, trade marks)

integration - the situation when more than one company choose to join or work together

integrative growth - extension by way of backward, forward or horizontal integration

interest - money paid to a lender for the use of borrowed money; or a stake in a business

interest rates - the cost of borrowing money, expressed as a percentage of the loan per period of time

interest-rate swap - an exchange between two parties, e.g. of fixed interest bonds for floating rate bonds, in an attempt to reduce risks or costs

interference - the negative way of describing governmental action in the economy

intermediaries - all the people or organizations in the marketing channel between producers and customers

intermediate goods - goods that will be further processed or transformed before being sold to consumers

internal audit - a control by a company's own accountants, checking for completeness, accuracy and deviations from standard accounting procedures

International Monetary Fund (the IMF) - receives **quotas** from members and lends these, and **special drawing rights**, to countries with balance of payments problems

international trade - the exchange (buying and selling) of goods and services between different countries

intervention - the neutral term to describe governmental action in the economy

in the black - to have a surplus, an excess of income over expenditure

in the red - to have a deficit, an excess of expenditure over income

intrinsic value - exists when the exercise price of a call option is below (or of a put option is above) the current market price of the underlying share

inventory - (especially US) an amount of goods stored ready for sale; in accounting, the value of raw materials, work in progress, and finished but unsold products

inventory turnover - the number of times the average inventory has been sold during a period

invest - to spend money in order to produce income or profits

investment - the purchase of materials, machines, property, securities, etc. in order to produce income or profits

investment bank - the American name for what the British call a merchant bank – one that arranges finance for industry, international trade, etc.

investment goods - see **capital goods**

investment grade - a rating given to a bond-issuing company by private ratings companies, according to its financial situation and performance

investment trust - a limited company (with a fixed share capital) that holds and deals in shares of other companies, to provide a low-risk income for its shareholders

investor - a person or organization that buys property or securities in order to receive an income or make a profit

invisible hand - according to Adam Smith, the mechanism that leads individuals, in selfishly pursuing their own interests, to achieve the best good for all

invisible trade - trade in services rather than tangible goods, e.g. banking, insurance, technical expertise

invoice - a list of goods or services received that serves as a bill

involuntary unemployment - when people seek paid employment but there are not enough jobs to be had

IS curve - traces the combination of interest rates and GNP at which investment equals saving

issue - to offer securities for sale to the general public; a quantity of securities offered to the public

issued share capital - the amount of capital that a company has sold at any particular time

issuing house - in Britain, a financial firm (usually a merchant bank) that specializes in finding buyers for new shares or bonds

jobless - unemployed (adjective and collective noun)

job-order cost accounting - determines the cost of an individual item or batch or job lot of assembled goods

journal - book in which transactions are recorded in the order that they take place

junk bond - high-yielding bond issued by less secure companies; also used to finance leveraged buy-outs

kerb market - an unofficial market in which securities are bought and sold, e.g. when the official stock exchange is closed

Keynesianism - the belief that government intervention in the economy is sometimes necessary as the market system does not automatically lead to full employment

labor union - see **trade union**

labour (GB) **or labor** (US) - paid work that provides goods and services

labour intensive - requiring a large amount of labour per unit of output, so that wages make up a large proportion of production costs

laissez-faire - the belief that the economy works best when the state does not interfere

land - the earth, and the raw materials contained in it or growing on it

last-in, first-out (LIFO) - method of inventory valuation that assumes that the most recently purchased or produced goods are sold first

launder - to process illegally-obtained money through more than one bank, in order to conceal its origin

law of diminishing marginal utility - additional units added to a consumer's stock of a commodity give progressively less satisfaction

law of diminishing returns - a decreasing amount of extra output is gained when extra units of a varying input are added to a fixed input

law of downward-sloping demand - demand generally decreases when prices increase

lay off - to dismiss from employment, sometimes temporarily

lease - the right to use property for a certain number of years in return for payment (verb and noun)

ledger - a book of accounts

legal person - by law, a limited company is described as a legal person, separate from the people who own it

lend - to allow someone to use a sum of money that will have to be paid back

lender - person or institution that lends money to someone else

lender of last resort - the central bank, that lends to commercial banks if they have no other means of borrowing

letter of credit - a paper issued by a buyer's bank as proof that the seller will be paid

leverage - see **gearing**

leveraged buy-out (LBO) - buying a company's shares with money borrowed on the security of the company's assets

levy - to impose and collect a tax or other financial charge

liabilities - money that a company will have to pay to someone else – bills, taxes, debts, interest and mortgage payments, etc.

liability insurance or **third party insurance** - protects the insured person (the first party) against his liability to pay compensation for injury, etc. to anyone else (the third party); the second party is the insurer

liberalism - the belief that self interest, competition and the price mechanism are adequate to regulate an economy

LIBOR - the London inter-bank offered rate, the rate at which commercial banks in London lend each other Eurodollars

licensing - selling the right to a manufacturing process, trademark, patent, etc., usually in a foreign market

limited company or **corporation** - one that is only liable for the amount of capital that shareholders have invested, and not for debts greater than this amount

limited liability - responsibility for debts up to the value of the company's share capital

liquid assets or **available assets** - anything that can quickly be turned into cash

liquidate - to sell personal assets in order to pay creditors

liquidation or receivership or **winding up** - the compulsory sale of the assets of a bankrupt company

liquidator or **receiver** or **administrator** - person appointed by a court who realizes (turns into cash) a company's assets in order to repay creditors

liquidity - cash and other liquid assets in excess of current liabilities; the ease with which an asset can be spent or sold

liquidity preference - the public's demand for money in cash or current bank accounts; money which is saved rather than spent or lent

listed or **quoted companies** - companies whose shares are traded on a stock exchange

list price - the manufacturer's or wholesaler's recommended price, before any discounts or special reductions are offered

Lloyd's - large international insurance market in London; an association of underwriters and brokers, trading in groups called syndicates

LM curve - shows the interest rates and income levels at which the supply and demand for money (liquidity preference) are equal

loan - something lent (usually money) that will have to be given or paid back (usually with interest)

long position - buying a security, either for investment purposes or in anticipation of future price rises

long run - the period of indeterminate length in which, in economic theory, all markets should readjust until they are in equilibrium

long-term financing - whether debt or equity, extends beyond five years

loophole - (pronounced loop-hole) a legal way of avoiding tax by exploiting part of a law

loss-leader pricing - selling a popular product at a loss, hoping to attract customers who will also buy other products

lower - to decrease (a price, tax rate, interest rate, etc.); also a comparative adjective (low, lower, lowest)

M0 - the wide monetary base, or high-powered money; all notes and coins in circulation and in banks, plus the banks' balances in the central bank

M1 - narrow money or transactions money; coins and notes and money placed in current accounts

M2 - broad money; a US measure including notes and coins plus time deposits (interest-bearing savings accounts)

M3 - M1 plus all time deposits (or savings accounts) in the banking system

M4 - M3 plus all the money deposited in building societies (GB) and savings and loan associations and money market funds (US)

macroeconomics - the study and analysis of the economy as a whole

mail order - purchasing goods by post, from a catalogue

managed floating or **dirty floating exchange rate** - one that does not float freely: if it rises or falls too much, the Central Bank will intervene in the markets

management buy-in - a management team from outside a company buys a majority of its shares, and then replaces the existing management

management buy-out - a group of managers, anticipating future profits, borrows money in order to buy the company they run from its shareholders

management letter - a letter addressed to a company's directors by the auditors, outlining deficiencies and suggesting improved operating procedures

managerial accounting - the elaboration of financial reports necessary to efficient management (on the cost of products, future plans, etc.)

marginal - in economics, means resulting from the addition of one more unit

marginal cost - the additional cost incurred by producing one more unit of a product

marginal product - the increase in output resulting from the use of an additional unit of an input or factor of production

marginal propensity to consume - the proportion of additional disposable income that is spent on additional consumption

marginal propensity to save - the proportion of additional disposable income that people choose to save

marginal revenue - the change in total revenue resulting from increasing sales by one unit

marginal utility - the additional satisfaction derived from consuming a further unit of a commodity

marine insurance - protects ships and their cargoes against loss or damage

market - the total demand for a good; the set of all actual and potential buyers of a good or service; the place where people buy and sell; the process by which buyers and sellers of goods, services and factors of production interact to determine prices and quantities

market/book ratio - a company's stock market value relative to the amount invested by shareholders

market challenger - the company with the second-largest market share

market economy - one in which prices and quantities are determined by supply and demand

market failures - situations in which free competition and the effects of supply and demand do not operate (e.g. monopolies and oligopolies, and externalities)

market follower - a small company in a market, which presents no threat to the market leader

market leader - the company with the largest market share

market-makers - wholesalers in stocks and shares who make a market (obliged to deal in all circumstances with brokers)

market price - the price of a share quoted at any given time on the stock exchange; the current price of a commodity, product, service, etc. in a competitive market

market price equilibrium - the price at which the amount that buyers wish to buy equals the amount that sellers wish to sell

market standing - a company's position in a market – whether it is the leader, a close challenger, or one of many market followers

market value - how much an asset would be worth if sold today

mark-up pricing - see **cost-plus pricing**

matching principle - the revenues generated in an accounting period are identified with related costs, whenever they were incurred

mature - to become due for payment

maturity - the date when the principal of a redeemable security (a loan, a bond, etc.) becomes repayable

McFadden Act - in the USA, restricts commercial banks to operating in only one state

medium term financing - matures within one to five years

Memorandum of Association (GB) or **Certificate of Incorporation** (US) - the document drawn up by a company's founders stating its name, purpose, registered office or premises and authorized share capital

mercantilism - the attempt to increase national wealth by building up a huge trade surplus, by exporting more than the country imports

merchandise inventory or **goods on hand** - includes raw materials and goods in process as well as unsold finished goods

merchandise trade - American name for what the British call visible trade: trade in goods

merchant - person who buys (and takes possession of) goods, and sells them on his or her own account

merchant banks - (in Britain) specialize in raising capital for industry, financing international trade, issuing securities, etc.

merge - to combine with another company (in a **merger**)

microeconomics - concerns the economic factors affecting individual consumers and companies

middlemen - a general term for agents, brokers, merchants, wholesalers, retailers, etc.

minimum wage - the lowest wage rate that any employer can legally pay, set by the government

minority interest - a shareholding in a company of which over 50% is owned by a holding company

mixed economy - one with both private and public sectors

mobility of labour - the degree to which workers are willing (or able) to move from one location or occupation to another

monetarism - the theory that prices and economic activity generally are determined by the quantity of money in circulation

monetary - (adjective) relating to money or currency

money - a means of payment, especially coins and banknotes, although some definitions also include bank deposits, cheques, etc. (see **M0, M1**, etc.)

money market - the inter-bank market in short-term instruments such as treasury bills, bills of exchange, etc.

money market fund - a fund that offers investors higher interest than normal deposit accounts in banks

money stock - the amount of money in circulation in an economy

money supply - the money stock multiplied by its velocity (the number of times it is spent in a given period)

money supply targets - limits to the growth of the money supply, set by governments following monetarist theory

monopolistic competition - situation in which there are only a few sellers

monopoly - situation in which there is only one seller of a product or service

monopsony - a buyers' monopoly, a situation in which there is only one buyer

moonlighting - working in a second job (perhaps in the evening, under the light of the moon) that is not declared to the tax authorities

mortgage - a loan, usually to buy property, which serves as security for the loan; to take out a loan with a property as security

most favoured nation clause in the GATT - means precisely that there must not be one – countries must offer the same conditions to all trading partners

multiple pricing - see **demand-differential pricing**

multiplier - the number of times an increase in government spending or investment increases GNP due to secondary consumption

mutual funds - see **unit trusts**

NAIRU or **non-accelerating-inflation rate of unemployment** - another name for the natural rate of unemployment

national debt - the total amount of money borrowed by a government and its predecessors, on which it has to pay interest

nationalized industry - one owned by the government, for economic, social or strategic reasons

natural monopoly - a monopoly in a market or field in which it would not be practical to have competition

natural rate of unemployment - in economic theory, the rate of unemployment which corresponds to optimal output and does not cause any inflation

negative yield curve - arises when short-term interest rates are higher than long-term ones

net assets - fixed assets plus the difference between current assets and liabilities

net book value - the value of an asset; under historical cost accounting, its purchase price minus accumulated depreciation charges

net national product - GNP minus an allowance for depreciation

net profit - the excess of all revenues and gains in a period over all expenses and losses

net realizable value - the amount that could be raised by selling an asset (less the costs of sale)

night safe - a safe set in the wall of a bank in which business customers can deposit money in the evenings and at weekends when the bank is closed

nominal GNP - the figure for gross national product that does not allow for inflation

nominal value or **par value** or **face value** - the amount written on a share certificate showing how much capital it represents

nominal yield of a bond - the rate of interest stated on the bond document

nominee - a person or company holding securities for someone else who wants to remain anonymous

non-current assets - those that will not be consumed or turned into cash, but will be retained for more than one accounting period

normative economics - deals with ethical issues and value judgements such as tax and welfare rates, the distribution of income, etc.

notes receivable and **notes payable** - on a balance sheet, refer to promissory notes: written promises to pay a stated amount at a given time

numbered account - secret bank account (largely in Switzerland) in which hardly anyone (or no-one) at the bank knows the account holder's identity

objectivity principle - (in accounting) all data recorded should be verifiable and free from bias

odd pricing or **odd-even pricing** - the practice of selling something at, e.g. 499 instead of 500, so that customers think of 400 rather than 500

off-balance-sheet transactions - financial business that need not be registered as loans on a balance sheet

offer - a bid; an amount offered; to propose something that can be accepted or refused

offshore banking - transactions by non-residents in foreign currencies in tax havens such as Bermuda, the Cayman Islands, Liechtenstein, etc.

off-the-shelf company - a ready-made company that can be bought from an agent, i.e. a company formed and held specifically for later resale

oil crisis - the situation for petrol-importing countries when the producing countries dramatically increased the price (in 1973 and 1979)

oligopoly - the situation in a market where there are only a small number of large suppliers

oligopsony - the situation in a market where there are only a limited number of buyers

operating margin - operating profit before the payment of interest and taxes divided by sales

operating profit or loss - net amount before adding or subtracting extraordinary items

opportunity cost - the amount that a factor of production could have earned if put to another use

option - the right but not the obligation to buy or sell a fixed quantity of a commodity, currency or security at a fixed price on (or in the US, until,) a particular date

ordinary shares (GB) or **common stock** (US) - fixed units of a company's share capital that usually pay a dividend and have voting rights

organized labour or **labor** - workers combined in trade unions (GB) or labor unions (US)

outlay - an amount of money spent on a particular project

outlet - a place where goods are sold to the public – a shop, store, kiosk, market stall, etc.

out-of-the-money - call options with an exercise price higher than the share's current market price; put options with an exercise price lower than the share's market price

output - the total value of the goods produced or services performed (by a person, a company, an industry, or a whole country)

outstanding - of a debt: unpaid, remaining to be paid; of a person or other entity: remarkable, excellent, superior, etc.

overdraft - an arrangement by which a customer can withdraw more from an account than has been deposited in it, up to an agreed limit; interest on the debt is calculated daily (**to overdraw**)

overdue - owing, late in being paid

overextended - describes a business owing far more than the value of its current assets

overheads (GB) or **overhead** (US) - the various expenses of operating a business that can't be charged to any one product, process or department

overheating - economic expansion at a rate that cannot be sustained

overproduction - when supply exceeds demand, which soon leads to cutbacks in production, unemployment, and a recession

oversubscribed (of a new share issue) - one for which there are more buyers than shares available

overtime - time worked in excess of an agreed number of hours per day or week

over-the-counter market - stock exchange for newer and smaller companies, and those that do not wish to meet all the major stock exchanges' rules

overtrading - a situation where a company tries to produce and sell goods with too little capital

owe - to have an obligation to pay or repay money

own - to have or possess

paid-in surplus - see **share premium**

paid-up capital - share capital that has actually been subscribed by shareholders

parent company - one that owns at least 50% of the ordinary shares of a subsidiary company

parity - another term for an exchange rate, or for par value

participation certificate - grants its holder part of the ownership (equity) of a company, but without voting rights

partnership - a business run collectively by two or more individuals, who share risks and profits

par value - see **nominal value**

patent - the exclusive right given to an inventor to produce, or to authorize others to produce, a new product or process

pay - money earned by employees for work performed, in the form of wages or salary

pay differentials - differences between wage rates paid to different classes of workers, depending on their skills, the danger of the job, etc.

payroll - a complete list of all a company's employees, with details of how much they earn

pay scales - the different rates of pay established for different categories of worker

peak - the highest point on the business cycle; to reach the highest point

peg - to fix the value of a currency against something else (another currency or a precious metal)

pension - a regular sum of money paid to a retired worker in return for past services or contributions

pension fund - financial institution that invests workers' pension contributions, and pays them pensions on retirement

perceived value pricing - considers customers' perceptions of price in relation to quality, durability, service, etc.

perfect competition - exists when there are a large number of sellers and buyers, freedom to enter and leave markets, a complete flow of information, etc.

permanent assets - see **fixed assets**

personal selling - the presentation of goods or services to potential customers by sales representatives

petrodollars - dollar deposits in the banking system coming from rich, oil-producing nations

Phillips Curve - used to be thought to demonstrate a trade-off (exchange) between unemployment and inflation

piecework - a method of paying workers according to the quantity of articles or pieces they produce

planned economy or **command economy** - one in which economic decisions (supply, prices, etc.) are made by the government rather than by market forces

plant - collective word for factories and the machinery inside them

poison pill - a defence against a raider: taking action which makes the company less attractive

policy - contract by which the insurer agrees to pay the insured a certain sum of money if or when certain stated events happen; plans determining a government or firm's actions

portfolio - the total of an investor's different investments

positive economics - is concerned with the description and analysis of economic facts

posting - entering items in account books or ledgers, from temporary records such as journals

preference shares or **preferred shares** (or **stock**) - receive a fixed dividend, which is paid before other shares get any dividend

premises - the place in which a company does business: an office, shop, workshop, factory, warehouse, etc.

premium - the money paid by the insured to the insurer in return for insurance cover or benefits payable; the positive difference between the current price of a security and its par value

prepaid expenses - amounts paid in advance and recorded as such on a balance sheet

prestige pricing - giving a high price (perhaps an excessively high price) to a luxury product to reinforce its luxury image

price - the cost of a good or service to the consumer

price discrimination - the sale of the same commodity to separate markets at different prices, usually by a monopolist

price/earnings ratio (PER) - the present market price of an ordinary share divided by the company's net earnings per share for the past year

price effect - the result of a change in the price level if consumers' income remains unchanged

price elasticity - the relationship between the price of a product and the quantity bought by consumers

price fixing - agreement among competitors to sell at the same price (which is illegal in many countries)

price leadership - the ability to influence prices in a particular industry or market

price war - reciprocal price cuts between competing suppliers in the attempt to gain a larger market share

pricing strategy - the choice of a product's initial and subsequent price range

primary sector of the economy - the extraction of raw materials from the earth, and agriculture

prime cost or **direct cost** - the sum of direct material costs and direct labour costs

prime rate - see **base rate**

principal - the amount of a loan, which the borrower has to pay back when the loan matures; a person who engages a broker to buy and sell for him

private limited companies - (in Britain) cannot offer shares to the public; their owners can only raise capital from friends, banks or venture capital institutions (see also **public limited company**)

private sector - businesses owned by private investors (as opposed to the government)

privatize or **denationalize** - to sell a publicly owned industry to private investors

process cost accounting - is used to determine the cost of continuously processed products, over a given time period

producer market - see **industrial market**

production function - the mathematical relation between the maximum output of a good and the amount of inputs needed to produce it

productivity - the amount of output produced in a certain period, using a certain amount of inputs

profit - the difference between the price received for a product and its cost (the price of the factors of production used to make it); excess of revenues over expenses; an entrepreneur's reward for using factors of production in economic activity

profitability - the ability of a business to earn profits (to be profitable), compared to competitors, for example

profit and loss account - (in Britain) financial statement which shows the profit or loss made by a company during the accounting period

profit margin - see **return on sales**

profit motive - the belief that the function of business is to make as much profit as possible

profit sharing - system in which an agreed proportion of a company's profits is paid to employees (as well as wages and salaries)

progressive taxation - is levied at a higher rate on higher incomes

pro-forma invoice - an invoice sent to a customer so that it can be paid before the goods are supplied

proprietary ratio - see **gearing**

prospectus - document inviting the public to buy shares, stating the terms of sale and giving information about the company

protectionism - the practice of restricting imports in order to increase the sales of domestic products

provisions - money set aside in the accounts (and charged against profits) to provide against expected losses such as bad debts

proxy - person granted power of attorney by a shareholder to vote for him or her at an annual general meeting

proxy fight - a way of gaining control of a company by persuading other shareholders to let you vote for them (as proxies) at the annual general meeting

prudence - see **conservatism**

prudential ratios - ratios between a bank's deposits and liquid assets that are considered sufficient to meet demands for cash

PSL2 (public sector liquidity 2) - the widest monetary aggregate used in Britain, which adds Treasury Bills and similar instruments to M4

public goods and services - those which are for the benefit of all citizens

public limited company (PLC) - a successful, established company that is allowed to offer its shares for sale on the open stock market

public sector - local government and nationalized industries or services

public spending - government expenditure (on health, education, social security, defence, etc.)

public utilities - services such as the provision of water, electricity, gas, etc.

purchase - another word for to buy

purchasing power or **buying power** - the amount of goods and services that money can buy at a given time

purchasing power parity - the rate of exchange between two countries at which the price of a representative basket of goods is the same

put option - the right to sell a fixed quantity of a commodity, security or currency at a certain price on a certain future date

quantity discount - a price reduction offered on the purchase of a large quantity

quick-asset ratio or **acid-test ratio** - liquid assets (including cash and accounts receivable) divided by current liabilities

quorum - a minimum number of directors and shareholders who must be present at a meeting in order for decisions to be taken

quota - a maximum amount of things allowed, e.g. a quantity of imports; a country's contribution to the International Monetary Fund

quotation - the current market price of a share on the stock exchange, or a statement of price for a particular quantity of goods

quote - to calculate and offer a price for something, a legally-binding estimate

quoted company - see **listed company**

raider - person or company that tries to obtain control of another company by buying its shares on the stock market

raise - to make something rise or increase (e.g. prices, tax rates); or to obtain capital

rally - an increase in stock prices, after a fall (to rally - to rise after a fall)

rate of return - the amount of profit, interest or dividend received from an investment, expressed as a percentage

ratio - the relation between two quantities expressed as the number of times one is greater than the other

rational expectations - the belief that people's expectations compensate for, and render useless, interventionist government policy

rationalize - to eliminate unnecessary employees, equipment, processes, etc. from a company or factory to make it more efficient

raw materials - minerals, metals, agricultural goods, etc. extracted from the ground and used in industry

real estate - US term for land and buildings; the British term is **property**

real GNP - nominal gross national product divided by the price index, to allow for inflation (also **real interest rate, real value, real wages**, etc.)

rebate - part of a payment that is given back (e.g. from taxes)

receipt - (the 'p' is not pronounced) a document showing that money has been paid or goods received

receivables - see **accounts receivable**

receiver - see **liquidator**

receivership - see **liquidation**

recession - a period during which economic activity (spending, investment) falls, and unemployment rises

recommended price - the price the manufacturer communicates to retailers, but which they are free to disregard

recovery - an increase in economic activity after a recession, or a rise in share prices

redeem - to repay a bond, debenture, mortgage, etc.

redemption yield or **maturity yield** - the amount of income received from a fixed interest security, including interest and its repayment value, expressed as a percentage of its current market price

reducing balance or **declining balance** or **diminishing balance method of depreciation** - writes off the same percentage (but consequently a smaller amount) of an asset's value each year

redundancy - the state of no longer being needed by an employer (**to be made redundant**)

reflation - government policy designed to increase economic activity, by increasing the money supply, or reducing taxation or interest rates (**to reflate**)

refund - money given back, usually because goods are defective (**to refund**)

registered share - one made out in the name of the owner, who is entered on the company's share register

Registrar of Companies - compiles companies' Memoranda and Articles of Association, and annual financial statements

regressive taxation - makes poorer people pay a greater proportion of their income in tax than the rich

regulation - governmental control of business, concerning safety, minimum wages, etc.

reimburse - to repay or pay back money to someone

reinsurance - the sharing of large risks among two or more insurers

remuneration - payment for work or services; another word for a salary (**to remunerate**)

rent - money paid for (or income received from) the use of land or buildings

repayment - partial settlement of a debt (perhaps at monthly or quarterly intervals)

reschedule - to increase the duration of a loan, to delay the time when it has to be paid back

research and development (R&D) - the search for new and improved products and processes

reserve assets of a bank - cash, deposits held by the central bank, Treasury bills, and other discountable securities

reserve currency - a relatively stable currency held by central banks that can be used in international trade, e.g. US$, DM, Yen

reserve requirements - the amount of money commercial banks are obliged to deposit with the central bank

reserves - money set aside out of profits, rather than distributed to shareholders; a central bank's holdings of gold, foreign currencies, and IMF drawing rights

residual unemployment - affects people who can be described as "unemployable"

resources - available stocks of raw materials, money, labour and other assets that a company can put to use

results - the profit (or loss) made by a company

retail banking - commercial banks' dealings with individual customers and small businesses

retailer - a merchant such as a shopkeeper who sells to the final customer

retail price index (RPI) (GB) or **consumer price index (CPI)** (US) - indices of inflation, weighted averages which measure the cost of essential goods and services

retail price maintenance (RPM) - when manufacturers can enforce a particular price for their products, and prevent retailers reducing it

retained earnings - profits that are not distributed to shareholders but reinvested or ploughed back (GB) or plowed back (US)

return on investment (ROI) - the amount earned in direct proportion to the capital invested

return on sales or **profit margin** - sales revenue minus all operating expenses divided by the number of sales

revaluation - the increase in the fixed exchange rate of a currency

revenue - see **income**

revenue principle or **realization principle** - revenue is realized at the moment when goods are sold (or change hands) or when services are rendered

rights issue - new shares issued by a company and offered to existing shareholders at less than their market price

rise - an increase or upward movement; an increase in salary (US: a raise in salary)

risk - the possibility of loss; the amount that one may lose when investing (**to risk, to take a risk**)

risk capital - see **venture capital**

roll over - to renew a loan when it matures, to delay paying it back

royalty, royalties - money paid to copyright owners and authors

running yield - see **flat yield**

safe(ty) deposit box - a secure box in a bank where customers can keep valuable objects

salary - a fixed regular payment made by employers, usually monthly, for professional or office work

sales analysis - the measurement and evaluation of actual sales, and their comparison with sales goals and targets

sales force - collective term for a company's salespersons (US) or salespeople (GB)

sales representative or **sales rep** or **salesman** or **salesperson** - someone who contacts existing and potential customers, and tries to persuade them to buy goods or services

sales tax - a tax on goods and services, a percentage of the retail price

save - to keep money for the future, rather than spending it by consuming goods

savings and loan association or **"thrift"** - the nearest American equivalent to the British building societies

savings function - a Keynesian term relating the level of saving and the level of income

scarcity - a shortage of something; insufficient supply to meet demand (so that something is **scarce**)

scrip issue - see **bonus issue**

seasonal unemployment - exists in trades or occupations where work fluctuates according to the time of year

SEC - the Securities and Exchange Commission, which supervises American stock exchanges

secondary market - a market on which second-hand bearer shares and bonds can be freely traded by their first and subsequent owners

secondary sector of the economy - manufacturing industry, in which raw materials are processed or transformed into finished products

securities - saleable papers, traded on stock exchanges, that yield an income (dividend, interest, etc.)

securitization - the process of selling packages of bank debts to third party investors as bonds

selling price - total cost (unit cost plus overheads and "risk reward") plus profit

separate-entity principle or **accounting-entity assumption** - a business is taken to be an accounting unit separate from its owners, creditors, etc.

service (a debt) - to make regular interest payments

services - activities offered for sale to customers, (advice, transport, banking, insurance, restaurants, hotel rooms, etc.)

settle - to pay a debt or bill or account

share (GB) or **stock** (US) - a security representing a portion of the nominal capital of a company

shareholder (GB) or **stockholder** (US) - the owner of a share or stock

shareholders' equity or **stockholders' equity** - the money subscribed to buy shares plus a company's retained profits

share premium (GB) **or paid-in surplus** (US) - money realized by selling shares at above their par or nominal value

shock - an unexpected event that has economic consequences

short position - selling options or other financial instruments, including those one does not actually possess, expecting to buy them later at a lower price to cover the sale

short run - the short period during which supply and demand are relatively fixed

short-term financing - involves debts which mature within a year

sleeping partner - one who invests money in a partnership but who takes no part in managing it

slowdown - another word for the beginning of a recession, a downswing of the business cycle, a contraction of the economy

slump - another word for a recession, a decrease in demand, output, etc.

socialism - economic theory or system in which production should be for the public good rather than private profit

sole trader - an individual proprietor, the simplest form of business, e.g. a shop or store owned and run by a single person

solvency - having sufficient cash when liabilities become due (**to be solvent**)

source and application of funds - see **funds flow statement**

special drawing rights (SDRs) - interest-paying loans from the IMF, made up of a "basket of currencies"

speculation - dealing in a commodity or financial asset in the hope of making a profit on changes in market values (done by **speculators**)

spillovers - externalities, expecially those resulting from public expenditure

spot markets - places where commodities, currencies and financial instruments are traded for immediate delivery

spread or **margin** - the interest rate differential between deposits and loans, from which banks make their profits

squeeze - an attempt to limit (but not totally freeze) increases in pay, profits, credit, etc.

stabilize - to attempt to keep something at the same level, to avoid fluctuations

stabilizers - automatic mechanisms that counteract the effects of the business cycle

stag - person who buys new share issues, hoping to resell them at a profit if the issue is oversubscribed

stagflation - the combination of stagnation and rising inflation, a development in the 1970s which classical economic theory could not account for

stagnant - describes an economy that is not growing, but remaining in a state of recession (or of **stagnation**)

stake - see **holding**

stakeholder - a person with money invested in a business

standard cost accounting - takes a pre-determined cost and applies it to all goods, whether sold or unsold

standard of living - the amount of goods and services that people can afford to buy with their income

standard operating procedures - a firm's established methods for recording business transactions

standing order - an instruction to a bank to pay fixed sums of money to certain people at stated times

statement - a document listing amounts of money owing or owed

sticky (of prices and wages, etc.) - inflexible, slow to react to changes in supply and demand

stimulate - to boost or increase economic activity

stock - US equivalent of the British word "share", and in Britain a block of shares with a nominal value of 100, or various kinds of fixed-interest securities; in Britain, goods stored ready for sale, raw materials, work in progress, and finished but unsold products (US: inventory)

stockbroker - a member of the stock exchange who can advise investors and buy and sell shares for them

stock dividend or **stock split** - US names for new shares issued to shareholders instead of a dividend

stock exchange - an organized market for the issue of new securities and the exchange of second-hand ones

stock option - a way of remunerating and motivating executives, by allowing them to purchase stock in the future at today's market price

stocktaking - the practice of counting, checking and listing all the assets held in a shop or warehouse

straight line method of depreciation - charges an equal sum each year, calculated by dividing the original cost by the number of years of expected useful life

strike price - see **exercise price**

structural surplus or **deficit** - the result of deliberate government policy: an increase or decrease of spending or taxation

structural unemployment - occurs when the skills of available workers do not match the jobs vacant

subsidiary - a company partly or wholly owned by a holding company or a parent company

subsidy - money given to producers who are unable to produce at market price, or who provide services that are socially necessary but unprofitable

subsistence wages - the minimum that allows workers to buy food, clothes, and shelter, but no more

substitution effect of higher prices - consumers substitute other goods for those whose prices have risen

substitution effect of higher wages - means that people are tempted to work longer hours

supplier - any person or business that sells materials or goods or other resources to producers of goods or services

supply - the willingness and ability to offer goods and services for sale

supply-side theory - belief that economic policy should concentrate on aggregate supply (or potential output)

surplus - an excess of income over expenditure, or something left over and not required

sustainable growth - increase in real per capita income, GNP, etc. (i.e. growth that does not generate inflation)

syndicates - see **Lloyd's**

synergy - the working together of two companies, etc. to produce an effect that is greater than the sum of their individual effects

takeover - the acquisition of one company by another (**to take over**)

takeover bid - the attempt to gain control of a company by offering to buy its shares at a higher price than the market price during a limited period

target - a goal or result aimed at

target pricing - setting a price to meet a target rate of return on total costs at an estimated sales volume

tariff - a tax charged on imports

taxation - the transfer of money from individuals and companies to finance government expenditure

tax accounting - calculating an individual's or a company's liabilities for tax

tax avoidance - the practice of reducing tax liabilities to a minimum by legal means (see also **tax evasion**)

tax deductible - describes business expenses, donations to charity, etc. that can be subtracted from taxable income

tax evasion - the practice of making false tax declarations (which is of course illegal)

tax haven - a financial centre offering low taxes to non-residents, in which multinational companies are encouraged to set up offices

tax loss - a way of avoiding taxation by bringing forward capital expenditure into a tax year

tax shelter - a way of reducing or postponing taxation, by spending income on a pension plan, a life insurance policy, etc.

tendering or **competitive bidding** - making an offer for a contract, without knowing what price competitors are offering

tertiary sector of the economy - services, including commerce, marketing, banking, communications, transport, health care, education, etc.

third party insurance - see **liability insurance**

thrift - see **savings and loan association**

tight money or **dear money** - is expensive money, when interest rates are high and loans are hard to obtain

time and a half - overtime paid at 150% of the normal wage

time-period principle or **accounting-period assumption** - financial data must be reported for particular (short) periods

trade - to buy and sell; buying and selling

trade barriers - ways of restricting the amount of imports

trade cycle - see **business cycle**

trade discount - price charged by manufacturers to wholesalers, and wholesalers to retailers, obviously below the retail price

trade-off - an exchange between two variables, such as quick sales and long-term growth, or unemployment and inflation

trader - person or organization that earns money by buying goods, commodities, securities, etc. and selling them at a profit

trade terms or **terms of trade** or **terms of payment** - conditions of payment: when goods have to be paid for, in what way, at what price, etc.

trade union (GB) or **labor union** (US) - association of employees that negotiates with employers to improve its members' incomes and working conditions

tranche - a segment of a capital issue offered for sale on a particular date; an instalment

transaction - a single business deal; a sale or purchase; or the crediting or debiting of an account

transactions velocity of the circulation of money - the number of times each unit of money is spent during a given period

transfer pricing - practice of multinational companies of selling components from a high tax country to a subsidiary in a low tax one at an artificially low price

traveling salesman - see **commercial traveller**

Treasury - British and American name for the government's economic and finance ministry

Treasury bill - a short-term (three-month) bill sold by the government to commercial banks, usually to regulate the money supply

Treasury bonds - in America, long-term government bonds

Treasury stock - in America, stock that a company has bought back from the public

trial balance - a test to see whether all the debits and credits in a set of account books match

trough (pronounced /trof/) - the lowest point on the business cycle, from which the only way to go is up

true and fair view - what British law requires a company's accounts to give

trust - a large combination of business organizations, possibly tending towards a monopoly

turnover - a business's total sales revenue

ultra-vires - an action that is "beyond the powers" of a company, as stipulated in its Memorandum and Articles of Association

uncalled capital - that part of a company's issued capital that has not yet been paid for by shareholders

undercapitalized - a company that does not have sufficient share-capital to support its volume of trading

underground economy - all employment and transactions on which tax is not paid (= **black economy**)

undersell or **undercut** - to sell goods more cheaply than competitors

undervalued - a company whose stock market value is less than that of its assets

underwrite - to guarantee to buy, or find buyers for, a security issue; to take on the risk of paying for losses in accordance with the conditions of an insurance contract

underwriter - an organization, usually a bank, that purchases a share issue, hoping to sell it to the public; an insurance company that undertakes to meet losses

unearned income - income from property (rents) and investments (interest and dividends) as opposed to wages or salaries

unemployed - (all the people) not working but looking for work

unemployment - the situation in which there are not enough jobs available for the people looking for them

unissued capital - that part of a company's authorized share capital that has not yet been offered for sale

unitary elasticity of demand - exists when a price cut produces such a small change in sales that total revenue remains unchanged

unit-of-measure principle - all transactions have to be accounted for and recorded in a single monetary unit

unit trusts (GB) or **mutual funds** (US) - organizations that place small investors' money in a variety of stocks and shares

universal banks - banks which combine deposit and loan banking with share and bond dealing, investment advice, etc.

unlimited liability - the legal obligation to pay all one's debts, if necessary by the sale of one's possessions

unlisted securities - stocks or shares of companies not listed on the main stock exchanges

upturn - the end of a recession, when an economy begins expanding again

value-added tax (VAT) - a sales tax collected at each stage of production, excluding the already-taxed costs from previous stages

variable - a quantity that is liable to change; the adjective describing such a quantity

variable costing - see **direct costing**

variable costs - depend on the volume of output produced by a business

venture capital or **risk capital** - money invested in a new business and thus open to a rather large risk of loss

vertical integration - a company's acquisition of either its suppliers or its marketing outlets (wholesalers or retailers)

visible hand - name sometimes given to governmental spending on defence, welfare, the infrastructure, the correction of market failures, etc.

visible trade - trade in tangible goods (as opposed to services)

volatile - likely to change rapidly and often (the noun is **volatility**)

volume - in business, the amount of trade done in a certain period

voluntary liquidation - when an organization chooses to stop trading, sell its assets, and pay its debts

voluntary unemployment - exists when people choose not to work, often because they cannot find jobs that pay enough money (e.g. more than social security benefits)

voting shares - those categories of shares that give their holders the right to vote at companies' AGMs

voucher - a receipt or document that supports or proves an item in an account

wage or **wages** - money earned for an hour's or day's or week's work (by shop and factory workers, etc.)

wage/price spiral - the situation in which inflation leads trade unions to demand wage increases which leads producers to raise their prices, and so on

Wall Street - the popular name for the New York Stock Exchange, or for all the financial institutions in and around this street

warehouse - a large building in which goods are stored by producers or wholesalers

warehousing - storing goods in warehouses; in finance, using other people to buy shares prior to a takeover bid

warrant - a security issued at the same time as a bond, giving the holder the right to buy the same company's equities at a given price from a certain date

warranty - another word for a guarantee

wasting assets - those which are gradually exhausted (used up) in production and cannot be replaced

wealth - the stock of money or goods that a person or country possesses

wealth tax - an annual tax in several European countries on the value of an individual's assets, over a certain level

weighted - (of elements in a price index, or currencies in a basket): considered according to their relative importance

welfare - condition of general well-being; and government spending designed to achieve this

white-collar worker - person who works in an office: i.e. most people working in finance (as opposed to **blue-collar workers**, who work in factories)

white knight - an alternative buyer that comes to the rescue (or is persuaded to rescue) a company from a threatened hostile takeover

wholesale - connected with buying and selling goods in large quantities

wholesale banking - banks' dealings (making loans, accepting deposits) with other banks and financial institutions

wholesaler - intermediary between producers and retailers, who stocks goods, and delivers them when ordered

windfall - an unexpected profit

winding up - see **liquidation**

window dressing - see **creative accounting**

wind up - to liquidate a failing business by selling its assets

withdraw - to take money out of a bank account

withholding tax - tax deducted at source from payments such as dividends

working capital or **funds** - the stock of money (cash and liquid resources) required by a business to continue producing or trading

working capital ratio - see **current ratio**

work in progress - partially manufactured goods

write off - to abandon a debt as bad or uncollectable (to recognize that it will never be paid)

wrongful trading - continuing to trade after it is obvious that there is no reasonable prospect of avoiding bankruptcy

yield - the rate of income an investor receives from a security; to produce or provide income

yield gap - the difference between the average yield on equities and on bonds

zero coupon bond - pays no interest, but is sold at a large discount and ultimately redeemed at face value, providing a capital gain

New terms are constantly coming into this specialist vocabulary field. If you meet new terms you think are useful, list them here.

British and American Terms

The following are some of the more obvious and important differences in terminology between British and American English in the area of finance.

British	American
Annual General Meeting (AGM)	Annual Stockholders Meeting
Articles of Association	Bylaws
authorized share capital	authorized capital stock
barometer stock	bellwether stock
base rate	prime rate
bonus or scrip or capitalization issue	stock dividend or stock split
bridging loan	bridge loan
building society	savings and loan association or "thrift"
cheque	check
company	corporation
creditors	accounts payable
current account	checking account
debtors	accounts receivable
gilts or gilt-edged stock	Treasury bonds
labour	labor
Memorandum of Association	Certificate of Incorporation
merchant bank	investment bank
ordinary share	common stock
overheads	overhead
profit and loss account	income statement
property	real estate
quoted company	listed company
retail price index (RPI)	consumer price index (CPI)
share	stock
share premium	paid-in surplus
shareholder	stockholder
shareholders' equity	stockholders' equity
stock	inventory
trade union	labor union
unit trusts	mutual funds
visible trade	merchandise trade

Answer Key

1.2 Saying Numbers

Section one: 1 nought point oh oh two; 2 oh one two four four, two four nine, oh seven one; 3 room eight oh four; 4 thirty degrees below zero; 5 two-nil to Juventus.

Section two: 1 three point four eight eight and three point four nine one; 2 zero point oh oh oh one; 3 thirteen pounds sixty; 4 fourteen fifty; 5 oh point two two five or oh point two two nine; 6 one ninety five; 7 fifteen point oh oh five not fifteen thousand and five.

Section three: 1 thirty percent of two hundred (and) sixty; 2 a half of one percent; 3 three-quarters of a percentage point.

Section four: 1 one hundred and seventy five, a hundred seventy five; 2 a thousand and one; 3 the year two thousand; 4 one in a million; 5 two billion not two million.

Section ten: 1 two hundred (and) fifty thousand pound loan; 2 two hundred year old house; 3 fifty thousand dollar loss; 4 fifteen pound salmon.

Section eleven: 1 two hundred (and) thirty-four thousand, five hundred (and) sixty-seven; 2 one billion, two hundred (and) thirty-four million, five hundred (and) sixty-seven thousand, eight hundred (and) ninety; 3 one point two three four; 4 zero point oh oh two three four per cent; 5 three point one four one five nine; 6 nineteen dollars fifty; 7 seven pounds ninety-five; 8 nineteen thousand nine hundred (and) ninety-nine; 9 one thousand nine hundred (and) ninety-nine years; 10 nineteen ninety-nine; 11 oh one two two seven, seven six four oh oh oh; 12 oh oh, three three, five six seven, three two, four nine; 13 Gee four, seven four four, four four oh; 14 nineteen oh five, nineteen eighty-seven; 15 MI two three four six six two, two hundred and twenty-five; 16 thirty times twenty-five equals/is seven hundred (and) fifty; 17 thirty divided by twenty-five equals/is one and a fifth or one point two; 18 x squared plus y cubed equals z (GB: zed; US: zee).

2.1 Company Law

1 sole trader; 2 partnership; 3 losses; 4 liability; 5 bankruptcy; 6 corporations; 7 creditors; 8 shares; 9 prospectus; 10 registered; 11 capital; 12 premises; 13 issue; 14 financial; 15 files.

2.2 Bookkeeping

Exercise 1: 1 journals; 2 posted; 3 ledger; 4 transferred; 5 double-entry; 6 debits; 7 credits; 8 trial balance; 9 transactions; 10 invoice; 11 receipt; 12 vouchers.

Exercise 2: 1 record; 2 made; 3 received; 4 entered; 5 balance or check; 6 retain; 7 check; 8 analyse (US: analyze).

2.3 Accounting

1 f; 2 g; 3 c; 4 b; 5 d; 6 e; 7 a.

2.4 Accounting Principles 1

Exercise 1: 1 b; 2 e; 3 a; 4 c; 5 f; 6 d.

Exercise 2: 1 separate-entity; 2 continuity; 3 historical cost; 4 time-period; 5 unit-of-measure; 6 revenue or realization.

2.5 Accounting Principles 2

Exercise 1: 1 c; 2 a; 3 d; 4 b; 5 e.

Exercise 2: 1 conservatism; 2 objectivity; 3 matching (and time-period); 4 full-disclosure; 5 consistency.

2.6 Types of Assets

1 liquid assets; 2 net current assets; 3 wasting assets; 4 current assets; 5 intangible assets; 6 net assets; 7 fixed assets; 8 current assets; 9 wasting assets; 10 fixed assets; 11 intangible assets; 12 liquid assets.

2.7 Depreciation

Exercise 1: 1 lose; 2 wear out; 3 deducted; 4 converting; 5 exist; 6 involve; 7 writes off; 8 increase; 9 spreads; 10 charges; 11 allow; 12 encourage.

Exercise 2: 1 replaced; 2 gains; 3 estimate; 4 scrap; 5 charged, deducted; 6 reducing; 7 maintenance; 8 tax.

2.8 Cash Flow

Exercise 1: 1 net; 2 reserves; 3 working; 4 reputation; 5 suppliers; 6 liquidity; 7 positive; 8 insolvent.

Exercise 2: 1 d; 2 a; 3 e; 4 b; 5 c; i cash received; ii working capital; iii extended credit; iv liquidity crisis; v net profit.

2.9 Financial Statements

Exercise 1: The most probable words are balance, bookkeeping, capital, equilibrium, flow, liabilities, overheads, reserves, turnover.

Exercise 2: 1 True; 2 False; 3 True; 4 True; 5 False (if you don't have a debtors total, for example, you probably aren't doing any business); 6 False; 7 True (this means the market price, of course, rather than the book price); 8 False; 9 True; 10 False.

Exercise 3: 1 a; 2 b; 3 d; 4 c; 5 f; 6 e.

2.10 Liquid Metaphors

Exercise 1: 1 pool; 2 pouring or flooding; 3 source, run out of; 4 dry up; 5 trickle down; 6 awash; 7 ebb and flow; 8 pouring or channelling; 9 drain; 10 pouring or channelling; 11 flowing; 12 swimming.

Exercise 2: 1 sank (to sink without trace); 2 fluid (to be fluid); 3 crest (to ride on the crest of a wave); 4 under (to go under); 5 plug (to pull the plug); 6 depth (to be out of one's depth).

2.11 Bankruptcy

Exercise 1: 1 c; 2 c; 3 b; 4 a; 5 a; 6 a.

Exercise 2: 1 bankrupt; 2 bankruptcy; 3 bankrupt; 4 bankruptcy; 5 bankrupt; 6 bankrupt.

2.12 Phrasal Verbs: Bad Debts

Exercise 1: 1 c; 2 b; 3 e; 4 f; 5 i; 6 h; 7 g; 8 d; 9 a. The two regular verbs are "plough" and "wipe".

Exercise 2: 1 write off; 2 wound up; 3 put up; 4 wiped out; 5 go under; 6 ploughed back; 7 built up; 8 deal with; 9 bringing about.

2.13 Auditing

Exercise 1: 1 accuracy; 2 deviations; 3 standard operating procedures; 4 external; 5 determine; 6 board of directors; 7 ratified; 8 shareholders/stockholders; 9 Annual General Meeting (AGM); 10 deficiencies; 11 a synonym; 12 transnational corporations; 13 checking; 14 directives; 15 implemented; 16 subsidiaries.

Exercise 2: 1 review/check/evaluate/control; 2 give/present; 3 report; 4 appoint; 5 recommend; 6 legal.

2.14 Annual General Meetings

Exercise 1: 1 Who is eligible to attend Annual General Meetings? 2 Are all the shareholders entitled to vote? 3 What is the purpose of an AGM? 4 What information do the shareholders receive beforehand? 5 What happens if shareholders cannot attend the meeting? 6 How many shareholders have to be represented for an AGM to take decisions?

Exercise 2: 1 shareholders, annual report; 2 approve; 3 elect, auditors; 4 dividend; 5 a proxy.

2.15 Cost Accounting

Exercise 1: 1 d; 2 g; 3 c; 4 a; 5 f; 6 i; 7 e; 8 h; 9 b.

Exercise 2: 1 allocating, variable; 2 overheads, costs or expenses; 3 raw materials.

2.16 Word Partnerships - Account

Exercise 1: 1 account holder; 2 accounting methods; 3 account day; 4 accounting equation; 5 accounts payable; 6 accounting principles; 7 accounting period; 8 accounting procedures; 9 accounts receivable; 10 accounting standards; 11 account book; 12 bank account; 13 current account; 14 deposit account; 15 cost accounting; 16 managerial accounting; 17 numbered account; 18 profit and loss account; 19 savings account; 20 tax accounting.

Exercise 2: 1 accounting procedures; 2 accounting methods; 3 numbered accounts; 4 accounting equation; 5 accounting period, account day; 6 profit and loss account; 7 Accounts receivable, accounts payable; 8 managerial accounting.

2.17 Review - Accounting 1

Exercise 1: Bookkeeping: double-entry, journal, ledger, posting, trial balance, voucher.

Accounting principles: consistency, going-concern, matching, prudence, separate-entity, unit-of-measure.

Depreciation: amortization, annuity system, reducing balance, scrap value, straight line method, writing off.

Financial statements: accounts payable, below the line, deferred liabilities, income statement, net profit, reserves.

Exercise 2: 1 below the line; 2 straight line method; 3 deferred liabilities; 4 unit-of-measure; 5 going-concern; 6 accounts payable; 7 income statement; 8 reserves.

2.18 Review - Accounting 2

Exercise 1: credit, fair, owe, fund, and, value, view, audit, defer, data, debit, tax, account, true, loss, flow, cash, accrue, income, revenue, debt, asset, budget, cost, balance

Exercise 2: 1 true and fair view; 2 debit; 3 accrue; 4 defer; 5 account; 6 balance; 7 audit; 8 budget.

3.1 Forms of Money

1 a; 2 a; 3 c; 4 a; 5 b; 6 c; 7 b; 8 b; 9 a; 10 c; 11 b; 12 a; 13 c; 14 c; 15 a; 16 c; 17 c; 18 a.

3.2 Borrowing and Lending

1 b; 2 a; 3 b; 4 a; 5 c; 6 b; 7 a; 8 b; 9 a; 10 c; 11a. money; b. borrower, lender; c. borrow, lend; d. credit.

3.3 Central Banking

Exercise 1: 1 function; 2 implement; 3 control; 4 fix; 5 act; 6 issue; 7 influence; 8 supervise.

Exercise 2: 1 reserve; 2 interest; 3 assets; 4 cash; 5 maturity; 6 liquid.

3.4 The Money Supply

Exercise 1: 1 monetarist; 2 prices; 3 velocity; 4 commercial; 5 tight; 6 bonds.

Exercise 2: 1 interest rates; 2 credit; 3 aggregate demand; 4 output; 5 unemployment; 6 inflation; 7 the exchange rate.

3.5 Commercial Banking

1 deposits; 2 customers; 3 lend; 4 accounts; 5 wages; 6 salary; 7 transfer; 8 current account; 9 withdraw; 10 cheque; 11 standing orders; 12 bank loan; 13 overdraft; 14 debt; 15 spread; 16 depositors; 17 optimize; 18 liquidity; 19 liabilities; 20 return.

3.6 Types of Bank

1 central banks; 2 commercial banks; 3 universal banks; 4 finance house; 5 merchant banks; 6 investment banks; 7 building societies; 8 supranational banks

3.7 Banking Products

1 current account; 2 cash dispensers; 3 standing order; 4 cheque; 5 credit card; 6 deposit account; 7 mortgage; 8 overdraft; 9 loan; 10 foreign currency; 11 pension, 12 investment advice.

3.8 Word Partnerships – Bank

1 bank account; 2 bank balance; 3 central bank; 4 bank clerk; 5 commercial bank; 6 bank deposit; 7 bank holiday; 8 investment bank; 9 bank manager; 10 merchant bank; 11 bank note; 12 off-shore banking; 13 retail banking; 14 bank robbery; 15 savings bank; 16 bank statement; 17 banking system; 20 wholesale banking.

3.9 Interest Rates

1 c; 2 a; 3 c and d; 4 c; 5 a and d; 6 b and c; 7 b; 8 a and b; 9 c; 10 a; 11 a; 12 d.

3.10 Eurocurrencies

1 d, q; 2 c, p; 3 j, s; 4 a, n; 5 h, l; 6 b, r; 7 i, o; 8 g, k; 9 f, t; 10 e, m.

3.11 Exchange Rates

Exercise 1: 1 g; 2 c; 3 e; 4 h; 5 b; 6 f; 7 a; 8 d.

Exercise 2: 1 peg; 2 revaluation; 3 convertibility; 4 floating; 5 speculators; 6 central.

3.12 Third World Debt

Exercise 1: 1 f; 2 e; 3 a; 4 d; 5 c; 6 h; 7 b; 8 i; 9 g.

Exercise 2: 1 interest; 2 principal; 3 indebted; 4 pay the interest; 5 fail to pay the interest or repay the principal; 6 rescue them financially; 7 renew it (to borrow again for a further period); 8 postpone the repayment; 9 abandon it as a bad debt that will never be paid.

3.13 Banking Verbs

Across: 1 borrow; 4 over; 5 lend; 7 honour; 9 stop; 10 roll; 12 cash; 13 last; 16 bail; 19 reimburse; 21 off; 22 write; 23 trade; 24 yield.

Down: 1 owe; 3 withdraw; 4 open; 6 deposit; 8 reschedule; 9 settle; 11 loan; 14 sever; 15 fix; 17 service; 18 resort; 20 issue.

3.14 Review - Banking Services

1 chequebook; 2 loans; 3 investment advice; 4 banker's draft; 5 night safe; 6 foreign exchange; 7 standing order; 8 transfer; 9 credit card; 10 mortgage; 11 overdraft; 12 deposit account; 13 letter of credit; 14 current account; 15 safe (or safety) deposit box.

3.15 Insurance

1 policy; 2 indemnify; 3 retires; 4 sums; 5 gilts; 6 insurance brokers; 7 commission; 8 underwritten; 9 affluent; 10 claims; 11 catastrophes; 12 huge.

3.16 Time Metaphors

1 running; 2 left; 3 waste; 4 wasting; 5 save; 6 spare; 7 worth; 8 invested; 9 lose; 10 allocate; 11 given; 12 spend; 13 take; 14 taken.

4.1 Ways of Selling 1

1 broker; 2 middlemen; 3 retailer; 4 outlet; 5 sales force; 6 wholesaler; 7 distributor; 8 customer; 9 merchant; 10 franchisee; 11 agent; 12 consumer.

4.2 Ways of Selling 2

Exercise 1: 1 end users; 2 premises; 3 outlet; 4 chain; 5 telephone; 6 sales reps; 7 industrial; 8 retailer; 9 authorized dealer; 10 franchise; 11 agent; 12 vending machines.

Exercise 2: 1a; 2c; 3d; 4f; 5b; 6e

4.3 International Trade

1 nations; 2 commodities; 3 balance of trade; 4 balance of payments; 5 barter or counter trade; 6 protectionism; 7 factors of production; 8 climate; 9 division of labour; 10 economies of scale; 11 tariffs; 12 quotas.

4.4 Imports and Exports

Exercise 1: 1 b; 2 a; 3 f; 4 g; 5 d; 6 e; 7 c; 8 h.

Exercise 2: 1 discount; 2 traded; 3 merchant; 4 lading; 5 debts.

4.5 Incoterms

1 j; 2 h; 3 i; 4 f; 5 a; 6 g; 7 c; 8 e; 9 b; 10 d.

4.6 Financing Foreign Trade

Exercise 1: 1 b; 2 d; 3 e; 4 a; 5 f; 6 g; 7 c.

Exercise 2: 1 produce, send, load, ship, collect; 2 draw up, present, accept, send, sell, honour; 3 letter of credit, bill of lading, commercial invoice, insurance certificate, bill of exchange.

4.7 Pricing

Exercise 1: 1 True; 2 True; 3 True; 4 True; 5 False; 6 False; 7 True; 8 True; 9 True; 10 True.

Exercise 2: 1 point; 2 production; 3 costs; 4 profit or sales; 5 market; 6 market; 7 pricing; 8 cost; 9 cost; 10 costs.

Exercise 3: The second summary is the most accurate and complete. The first summary is incomplete, and the second and third sentences are misleading. The third sentence of the third summary is totally false.

4.8 Pricing Strategies

1 g; 2 h; 3 a; 4 b; 5 d; 6 c; 7 f; 8 e.

4.9 Word Partnerships – Price

Exercise 1: 1 price control; 2 cost price; 3 price cut and adjective cut-price; 4 price discrimination; 5 price elasticity; 6 exercise price; 7 price fixing; 8 price freeze; 9 going price; 10 historical price; 11 price index; 12 price list and list price; 13 price maintenance; 14 market price; 15 price mechanism; 16 minimum price; 17 price range; 18 recommended price; 19 price reduction; 20 retail price; 21 price rise; 22 selling price; 23 price sensitivity; 24 strike price; 25 price war; 26 wholesale price.

Exercise 2: 1 list price; 2 price war; 3 wholesale price; 4 historical price; 5 price index; 6 cost price; 7 price elasticity; 8 price control and price freeze; 9 price fixing and price maintenance; 10 exercise price and strike price.

4.10 Word Partnerships - Cost

Exercise 1: 1 cost accounting; 2 cost advantage; 3 average cost ; 4 carrying cost; 5 current cost ; 6 direct cost ; 7 factory cost ; 8 fixed cost ; 9 historical cost ; 10 indirect cost ; 11 labour cost ; 12 cost leadership; 13 marginal cost; 14 opportunity cost; 15 cost price; 16 prime cost; 17 replacement cost; 18 total cost; 19 unit cost; 20 variable cost.

Exercise 2: 1 historical cost; 2 current cost; 3 direct cost; 4 fixed costs; 5 variable costs; 6 cost price; 7 cost leadership; 8 marginal cost; 9 opportunity cost ; 10 carrying cost.

4.11 Review - Trade and Commerce

1 outlets; 2 distributor; 3 exchange; 4 end-user; 5 wholesaler; 6 elastic; 7 channel; 8 middlemen; 9 direct cost; 10 customer; 11 payments; 12 skimming; 13 overheads; 14 tariffs; 15 merchant; 16 penetration.

5.1 Stocks and Shares 1

Exercise 1: 1 True; 2 False; 3 True; 4 False; 5 False; 6 True; 7 False; 8 True; 9 True; 10 True.

Exercise 2: 1 floating; 2 underwrite; 3 quoted; 4 settled; 5 nominal, face or par value; 6 market price.

5.2 Stocks and Shares 2

1 shareholders; 2 bulls; 3 bears; 4 stags; 5 stockbrokers; 6 market-makers; 7 insiders; 8 arbitrageurs.

5.3 Types of Shares

1 equities; 2 ordinary shares; 3 participation certificates; 4 preference shares; 5 deferred shares; 6 blue chips; 7 barometer stocks; 8 growth stock; 9 defensive stock; 10 mutual fund.

5.4 Market Price Idioms

1 a; 2 d; 3 c; 4 b; 5 c; 6 d; 7 d; 8 c; 9 c or d; 10 c or d; 11 c; 12 c or e; 13 c or e; 14 d; 15 a; 16 d; 17 b; 18 d; 19 a; 20 c; 21 d; 22 d; 23 e; 24 b; 25 a; 26 b; 27 a; 28 a; 29 d; 30 a or b.

5.5 Rise and Fall

Exercise 1: Rise = advance, be firm, be strong, jump, leap, rally, rebound, recover, revive, and rocket. Fall = be weak, dip, drift, drop, ease, plummet, plunge, sink, slip, slump, tumble.

To rise after falling: rally, rebound, recover, revive.

Exercise 2: 1 arisen; 2 raised; 3 risen, rise; 4 rose; 5 raised; 6 raise; 7 arose or arises; 8 arise.

5.6 Bonds

Exercise 1: 1 h; 2 j; 3 d; 4 a; 5 b; 6 e; 7 i; 8 k; 9 g; 10 f; 11 c.

Exercise 2: 1 issue; 2 secondary; 3 coupon; 4 fixed; 5 yield; 6 above par; 7 maturity; 8 investment grade.

5.7 Financial Instruments

1 commercial paper; 2 zero coupon bonds; 3 detachable warrants; 4 securitization; 5 junk bonds; 6 interest-rate swap; 7 futures contract; 8 certificates of deposit; 9 off-balance-sheet transactions; 10 forward contract; 11 participation certificates; 12 currency swap.

5.8 Futures and Options

Exercise 1: 1 True; 2 False; 3 False; 4 True; 5 False; 6 True; 7 True; 8 False; 9 True; 10 False.

Exercise 2: call option, financial market, financial instrument, forward contract, forward market, futures market, market price, primary market, raw materials, spot market, spot price, strike price, etc.

Exercise 3: call option - put option; discount - premium; drought - flood; exercise price - market price; futures market - spot market; hedging - speculation; in-the-money - out-of-the-money; obligation - right.

5.9 Bonds and Shares

Bonds: above par, coupon, debt, floating rate, interest, investment grade, junk, maturity, redeem, zero coupon. Shares: accounting period, blue chip, broker, bull, crash, dividend, Dow-Jones, equity, flotation, insider. Both bonds and shares: convertible.

5.10 Review – Securities

1 bull, bear, stag; 2 gilt, option, future, stock, share, bond; 3 trade, deal, write, put, invest, call, buy, hedge, issue, sell; 4 dividend, return, interest, yield.

5.11 Review – Financial Instruments

1 preference share; 2 unlisted security; 3 bonus issue; 4 warrant; 5 junk bond; 6 zero coupon bond; 7 option; 8 swap; 9 gilt; 10 treasury bill; 11 ordinary share; 12 bearer share; 13 growth stock; 14 mortgage; 15 blue chip; 16 common stock; 17 deferred share; 18 debenture; 19 future; 20 rights issue.

5.12 Financial Ratios

1 dividend cover; 2 current ratio; 3 earnings per share; 4 quick ratio or acid-test ratio; 5 debt/equity ratio; 6 PER; 7 market/book ratio; 8 interest cover; 9 return on equity; 10 profit margin or return on sales; 11 return on total assets; 12 productivity.

5.13 Takeovers

1 reinforcing; 2 reducing; 3 rationalizing; 4 optimizing; 5 diversifying; 6 searching; 7 grow; 8 launch; 9 buy; 10 increase; 11 persuade; 12 sell; 13 friendly; 14 hostile; 15 board; 16 poison pill; 17 white knight.

5.14 Phrasal Verbs – Takeovers

Exercise 1: 1 h; 2 m; 3 g; 4 b; 5 k; 6 j; 7 e, 8 f; 9 n; 10 l; 11 d; 12 i; 13 o; 14 c; 15 a.

Exercise 2: 1 take over; 2 looking forward to; 3 cash in on; 4 fight off; 5 made up; 6 adhered to; 7 got away with; 8 rely on; 9 look after; 10 built up; 11 acted on; 12 take up; 13 fell through; 14 drawing up; 15 branch out.

5.15 Word Partnerships – Capital

Exercise 1: 1 capital asset; 2 capital expenditure; 3 capital formation; 4 capital gains; 5 capital goods; 6 human capital; 7 capital-intensive; 8 capital investment; 9 issued capital; 10 capital market;

11 nominal capital; 12 capital ratio; 13 share capital; 14 capital sum; 15 capital transfer; 16 capital turnover; 17 uncalled capital; 18 unissued capital; 19 venture capital; 20 working capital.

Exercise 2: 1 capital goods; 2 capital intensive; 3 uncalled capital; 4 capital transfers; 5 capital gains; 6 human capital; 7 unissued capital; 8 venture capital; 9 working capital; 10 capital asset.

5.16 Leveraged Buyouts

Exercise 1: 1 b; 2 g; 3 d; 4 h; 5 f; 6 a; 7 e; 8 c.

Exercise 2: 1 borrowed; 2 financed; 3 stock market value; 4 asset-stripping; 5 conglomerates.

5.17 Insider Dealing Puzzle

The British banker flies a helicopter; the Swiss banker finances international trade.

5.18 Business People

1 entrepreneur; 2 broker; 3 arbitrageur; 4 auditor; 5 cambist; 6 accountant; 7 economist; 8 market-maker; 9 sole trader; 10 liquidator; 11 actuary; 12 raider.

6.1 Basic Economic Terms 1

1 factors of production; 2 externalities; 3 microeconomics; 4 equilibrium; 5 econometrics; 6 macroeconomics; 7 aggregate demand; 8 gross national product (GNP); 9 endogenous; 10 exogenous.

6.2 Basic Economic Terms 2

1 economic; 2 fiscal; 3 economical; 4 inflation; 5 scarcity; 6 capital; 7 cost of living; 8 standard of living; 9 balance of payments; 10 protectionism; 11 fluctuate; 12 economize.

6.3 Describing Graphs

Graph 1: Answers marked with an asterisk (*) are only one of several possibilities: 1* significant improvement; 2 a peak; 3* substantial decline; 4 downward; 5* fall sharply; 6* improved dramatically; 7* falling off.

Graph 2: Answers marked with an asterisk (*) are only one of several possibilities: 1* fell dramatically; 2 by; 3* slipped; 4* levelled off; 5* went down; 6* rapid; 7 from; 8 to; 9 of.

6.4 The Business Cycle

Exercise 1: 1 depression; 2 expanded; 3 upturns; 4 downturns; 5 boom; 6 peak; 7 recession; 8 contracted; 9 recovery.

Exercise 2: Possible answers include: 1 fell dramatically . . . as a result of; 2 declined . . . because; 3 rapid growth . . . owing to; 4 fell . . . as a consequence of.

6.5 The Three Sectors of the Economy

Exercise 1: 1 c; 2 h; 3 e; 4 g; 5 d; 6 a; 7 b; 8 f.

Exercise 2: 1 extracted, consumed, transformed. 2 Various answers are possible, including distributed, transported, insured, warehoused and advertised.

6.6 Phrasal Verbs – Recession

Exercise 1: 1 j; 2 h; 3 b; 4 q; 5 n; 6 f; 7 l; 8 c; 9 d; 10 o; 11 k; 12 p; 13 g; 14 r; 15 i; 16 m; 17 e; 18 a.

Exercise 2: 1 level off; 2 fell off; 3 close down; 4 lay off; 5 looking for; 6 looked through; 7 take on; 8 cut back on; 9 set up; 10 pull out of; 11 scale down; 12 carried out; 13 put off; 14 bringing out; 15 carry on; 16 mark up; 17 count on; 18 bottomed out.

6.7 Political Economy

1 mixed economy; 2 austerity; 3 public sector; 4 market failures; 5 laissez-faire; 6 deregulation; 7 demand management; 8 intervention; 9 infrastructure; 10 crowd out.

6.8 Competition

1 c; 2 c; 3 b; 4 c; 5 a; 6 a; 7 a; 8 c; 9 b; 10 b.

6.9 Government Spending

1 g, l; 2 f, k; 3 d, t; 4 e, q; 5 a, n; 6 i, r; 7 b, o; 8 c, p; 9 j, s; 10 h, m.

6.10 Inflation

1 excess; 2 supply; 3 hyperinflation; 4 employment; 5 unemployment; 6 producers; 7 deflation; 8 spending; 9 restrictions; 10 consumer; 11 weighted; 12 interest; 13 debts; 14 assets.

6.11 Unemployment

1 seasonal; 2 voluntary; 3 frictional; 4 classical; 5 cyclical; 6 structural.
1 structural; 2 seasonal; 3 classical; 4 voluntary; 5 cyclical; 6 frictional.

6.12 Taxation

1 b; 2 a; 3 b; 4 b; 5 b; 6 a; 7 b; 8 b; 9 c; 10 c; 11 a; 12 b.

6.13 Word Partnerships - Tax

Exercise 1: 1 tax accounting; 2 tax allowance; 3 tax authority; 4 tax avoidance; 5 tax consultant; 6 corporation tax; 7 tax deductible; 8 direct tax/taxation; 9 tax evasion, 10 tax free; 11 tax haven;

12 income tax; 13 indirect tax/taxation; 14 tax inspector; 15 tax loophole; 16 tax loss; 17 taxpayer; 18 progressive tax/taxation; 19 tax rates; 20 tax rebate; 21 regressive tax/taxation; 22 tax return; 23 sales tax; 24 tax shelter; 25 withholding tax; 26 tax year.

Exercise 2: 1 are liable; 2 deduct, pay; evading; 3 avoid; 4 lower; 5 raise; 6 levies.

6.14 Economic Theories

Exercise 1: 1 Keynes; 2 Friedman; 3 Lucas; 4 Smith.

Exercise 2: 1f; 2d; 3g; 4a; 5i; 6h; 7j; 8b; 9e; 10c.

Exercise 3: 1 classical; 2 flexible; 3 market; 4 consume; 5 counter; 6 taxation; 7 stabilize; 8 inflationary; 9 anticipate; 10 aggregate.

Exercise 4: 1e; 2d; 3b; 4i; 5a; 6h; 7g; 8j; 9c; 10f.

Exercise 5: 1 decelerating; 2 unintended; 3 disprove; 4 undesirable; 5 unnatural; 6 destabilize; 7 ineffective; 8 imperfect; 9 unstable; 10 inefficiency; 12 unpredictable; 12 involuntary.

6.15 Income

1 salary; 2 purchasing; 3 differentials; 4 earn; 5 income; 6 standard; 7 cost; 8 distribution; 9 rent; 10 profits; 11 Progressive; 12 inequality.

6.16 Pay

1 pay-roll; 2 remuneration; 3 bonus; 4 incentive; 5 golden handshake; 6 salary; 7 pension; 8 pay scales; 9 minimum wage; 10 pay differentials; 11 wages; 12 overtime; 13 time and a half; 14 double time.

6.17 Review - Opposites

1 debited; 2 withdraw; 3 nationalized; 4 loss; 5 peak; 6 exogenous; 7 fixed; 8 appreciated; 9 wholesale; 10 liability.

6.18 Review - Economics 1

Business cycles: boom, depression, downturn, peak, recession, slowdown, slump, trough.

Competitive theory: barriers to entry, cartel, economies of scale, imperfect competition, monopsony, natural monopoly, oligopoly, spillovers.

Inflation: cost-push, demand-pull, excessive demand, index-linked, money supply, price level, real GNP, wage/price spiral.

International trade: autarky, balance of payments, barter, comparative advantage, exports, protectionism, quotas, tariffs.

6.19 Review - Economics 2

stagflation, recession, crowd out, GNP, employ, fiscal, trough, tax, market, economist, scarce, Keynesian, stimulate, peak, shock, economic, demand, downtown, money, index, marginal, supply, tight, boom, cycle, growth

6.20 Growth Metaphors

Exercise 1: 1 green; 2 blossoming (or flourishing); 3 fertile; 4 flourishing; 5 fruit; 6 sprouted; 7 grew; 8 sowing; 9 reap; 10 weed out; 11 branches; 12 GB: ploughing, US: plowing; 13 roots; 14 spreading; 15 branching out.

Exercise 2: 1 +ve; 2 -ve; 3 -ve; 4 +ve; 5 -ve; 6 +ve; 7 -ve; 8 +ve; 9 -ve; 10 +ve; 11 -ve; 12 +ve.

6.21 Word Chains

1. net profit – profit opportunity – opportunity cost – cost accounting

2. marginal cost – cost price – price maintenance – maintenance department

3. risk capital – capital market – market price – price index

4. limited corporation – corporation tax – tax loss – loss leader

5. retail sales – sales tax – tax accounting – accounting procedures

6. bull market – market share – share index – index linked

7. unearned income – income tax – tax free – free enterprise

8. merchant bank – bank account – account book – book value

Business Books from LTP

BOOKS FOR STUDENTS

Build Your Business Vocabulary
906717 87 6

John Flower

The ideal book to supplement most business English courses. Graded exercises in a comprehensive range of business areas. Self-study or class use.

Business Language Practice
0 906717 54X

John Morrison Milne

More comprehensive language work – business grammar, vocabulary, speaking, reading, writing. Lots of varied exercises.

Business English
0 906717 97 3

Peter Wilberg and Michael Lewis

Unique course material in looseleaf format providing frameworks for students and teachers to cooperate in a completely individualised programme. Also available as a bound book (ISBN 0 906717 72 8)

Business English Assessment
0 906717 96 5

Peter Wilberg

Flexible test which can be used as a placement or diagnostic test or at the end of a course as a progress test.

Business Partners
0 906717 81 7

Pearson Brown and John Allison

A lower intermediate course for both pre- and in-service students. An easy-to-use adult course with an emphasis on the real spoken language of business.

Business Matters
1 899396 10 1

Mark Powell

An upper intermediate course for serious students of business English which really gets to grips with what students need to learn at that level. Stimulating texts, huge variety of exercises, and realistic fluency work.

Basic Telephone Training
0 906717 42 6

Anne Watson-Delestrée

A unique package of book plus cassette, designed for beginners, but usable by any students who need to sharpen their telephone skills.

The Language of Meetings
0 906717 46 9

Malcolm Goodale

A lively course in the language of international meetings. A fully developed course with extensive practice material.

BOOKS FOR TEACHERS

Business Games
0 906717 58 2

Jenny Mawer

A photocopiable resource book containing business problems, issues, and ethics – to promote lively classroom discussion.

Meetings
0 906717 58 2

Malcolm Goodale

10 photocopiable simulations based on authentic reading texts.

One to One
0 906717 61 2

Peter Wilberg

Essential reading for all teachers of business English who are working or intend working in the one-to-one situation. Theoretical, but full of practical ideas.